CREATING REALITY

CREATING REALITY

A Guide to Personal Accomplishment

By Anthony C. Gruppo

ISBN 0-9660315-3-9 (pbk.)
PUBLISHED BY: CUTTER ENTERPRISES • PENNSYLVANIA

Creating Reality
A Guide to Personal Accomplishment
Anthony C. Gruppo

ON REALITY

People who have the ability to create reality often are those who have accomplished dreams and improved the quality of life for others.

ON DRIVE

We can remove any stain of spilled failure if we scrub it out with a circular motion of dedication and a blue collar work ethic.

ON GOALS

We need a road map that helps us reach our goals and achieve what others may see as unattainable.

ON MOTIVATION

Change is for everyone but evolution is for the motivated.

ON LEADERSHIP

You can monitor a leader's pulse rate by goals per minute.

ON THE FUTURE

Our past must ensure our future or success will never come to the present.

ABOUT THE AUTHOR

A s a young man, Anthony dreamed, as most young men do, of becoming rich and powerful, and lived each day driven by those goals. He soon learned that there is a significant difference between having money and power and the achievement of success and greatness.

Armed with the heart of a child, the mindset of a warrior and the vision of being successful, Anthony began a twenty-year odyssey from college dropout/construction worker to one of the most recognized and well-respected human service advocates. His compassion and tireless efforts on behalf of the clients he serves has made him a respected leader in his field.

In Creating Reality, Anthony shares with his readers the forces, experiences, lessons and individuals that shaped his life and helped make him successful. Let Anthony's road map of experience, vision and unique perspective give you the direction to *Create Reality*.

Anthony C. Gruppo is Senior Vice President and a member of the Board of Directors of Henry S. Lehr, Inc. and has been with the organization since 1980. He holds a B.S. degree in Business Administration.

Anthony is a nationally known speaker and presents seminars in motivation, marketing, negotiations, risk management, managed care and quality assurance. Anthony is the co-author of the "Infranet Model", a managed care textbook for providers of children's services. He is the creator and designer of various state and national association programs. Anthony formed the Apollo Consulting Alliance, serving the needs of behavioral healthcare organizations. He also founded the Lehr Institute, an education facility, training professionals in advanced risk management interventions. Anthony has instructed at the collegiate level on the "Psychology of Leadership" and serves on several boards of non-profit organizations.

An advocate of children, Anthony has twice received the "Friend of Children Award" given by the National Association of Homes and Services for Children.

Anthony C. Gruppo can be reached at c/o Henry S. Lehr, Inc., 3893 Adler Place, Bethlehem, PA 18017. Phone: 1-800-634-8237.

THE DEDICATION

Tara and Anthony, I have dedicated this book to you. You have the ability to achieve greatness beyond your young imaginations. It is my desire that you will support each other and guide the family in the future. You are a constant source of strength and courage and I will forever love and respect you. Your dreams are your path to success and happiness. Wherever your path leads, I will always stand with you. You can lead yourself to greatness because you are truly great children.

> With Love,
> Dad

CONTENTS

	Foreword
I	Creating Reality
II	The Stone Cutter
III	The Pinnacle of Greatness
IV	Mission Possible
V	Personal Dynamic Marketing Plan
VI	Dream Riders
VII	Personal Board of Directors
VIII	Your Opposite Hand
IX	Faith
X	Fear – The Total of Lost Moments
XI	Rainmakers
XII	The Non-Profit Professional
XIII	Honor the Humanity
XIV	The Donation of Motivation
XV	Attack
XVI	Corporate Juvenile Delinquents
XVII	People We All Know
XVIII	Corporate Kindergarten

XIX	A Checklist for the Future
XX	Expectations and Objections
XXI	The Pony Express Rides Again
XXII	Salesperson Anonymous
XXIII	The Hard Hat Club
XXIV	Scoring a Goal
XXV	The Lead in Leadership
XXVI	Handling Monkeys
XXVII	Leading a Successful Team
XXVIII	Building an Orientation Team
XXIX	Are They Better for Having Met You?
XXX	Rob Routine to Reach Reality
XXXI	The Inner Kill
XXXII	The Velveteen Executive
XXXIII	The Race
XXXIV	The Fall to Forever

FOREWORD

I believe a fear most leaders have is that someday we will lose our edge, our effectiveness and, perhaps, our ability to lead. Often we forget how we came to achieve what we have; we tend to drift and lose our focus. I wrote this book for selfish reasons. I was afraid of someday losing my way, my sense of motivation, focus and drive and running the risk of being replaced in the professional world I love.

I thought back to 1981, when I had received a Christmas present from my long time friend and mentor, Fred Miller. When I was promoted to a management position, Fred gave me a silver business card case which was engraved on the back simply "I HAVE ARRIVED". I'll never forget how easy it was to arrive, but how difficult it has been to stay.

I hope this book will help those who at one time or another, may lose their way. It is a blueprint for us to rebuild our structure. It concentrates on leadership, motivation and attitude, it's a journey that starts from the time we are young until we grow old. If you, the reader, ever lose your way, I hope this book guides you back. As long as we stay focused and remember how we built what we have, we can continue to lead and stay successful; but, in the event I ever lose my way, I intend to pull this off the shelf and find my way back.

– Anthony C. Gruppo

I

CREATING REALITY

I

CREATING REALITY

S uccessful people know that they create their own reality. We build the structure for personal motivation and create the fuel for self-starting machinery. Motivation and leadership begin within the person; marketing is an extension of our personality played to the music of our professions.

Leadership, marketing and motivation are keys to your success and ability to lead others. This book was written to serve as your guide to develop the mindset necessary for achievement and provide insight to follow your dreams and accomplish your goals.

Whether your role is parent, professional or partner, "Creating Reality" is a resource to explore the pathway to new challenges.

I decided to write this book because I believe that, as professionals or parents, almost anything is possible if we enter into the art of creating reality and the understanding of what motivates and makes us successful.

In 1977, I was a repo-man and bill collector for a local loan company and insurance agency. It was a beautiful afternoon and I was sitting in a Pontiac Grand Prix trying to start the vehicle to repossess it from the owner. I heard a knock on the driver's side window and looked over. There was the owner of the vehicle standing with a gas cap in the one hand and a cigarette lighter in the other. He informed me that if I would not get out of the car and return it to him, he intended to throw the cigarette lighter into the gas tank.

Having gone to repossess a pickup truck, I found that the brake lining had been cut. I chased into trailer parks and homes to find children eating pet food off the floor. It was then I realized that reality is different for everyone. I also realized the road to personal accomplishment travels through a tunnel of reality lit by hard work, dedication and a passion to make a difference to myself and others.

People who have the ability to create reality often are those who have accomplished dreams and improved the quality of life for others.

I remember one day after having come back from trying to locate delinquent customers and collect money, there was a meeting being held for the insurance salespeople. Another collector and I were asked to go down to a local store and pick up donuts and coffee for the insurance salespeople. On other occasions we were asked to clean the basement

4

when it had been damaged by underground water. We were given chores that made us feel that we were less than the other professionals in the office. In a frame, I still have my first paycheck from my collection days. The amount of the check was a net of ninety-eight dollars. The salary of a college dropout/construction worker turned repo-man.

My reality was much different than it was for others. Reality for me was hanging out in bars trying to make friends with members of society who could help me locate certain people I was looking for. Attempting to follow people, I would work late into the night. One of my favorite tactics was to go back to their high schools and locate their high school yearbooks because I found that people rarely change their patterns. I found to locate them, I could check their hobbies in high school and go into neighborhoods where they were living. They were still doing those same hobbies and that helped me locate them with their same friends. Later I would realize that complacency did not occur only in the corporate world among executives in the workforce, but that complacency was prevalent throughout the community, in all walks of life.

One of my favorite "jobs" was to repossess a late model Corvette. The owner was known to visit a local bar. I made friends with him after a few months and then asked if I could have a ride home. Looking at the car and admiring how wonderful the car was and how great it must be to own a Corvette, I asked if I could drive it. Of course he agreed, and, before he could get into the passenger side, I was gone with the vehicle. Creating reality became a way of life for me. It was an opportunity to succeed and win over people who were out to beat my employer on loan payments.

I was fascinated by how we were treated. When we went to parties or other social events and indicated that we were bill collectors, I noticed how negatively people reacted; they would not want to talk to us. In fact, I remember my associates asking that I not tell people that I was a bill collector. In fact, when asked what I did for a living, they would tell people I was a financial advisor.

One particular day my employer, who also owned an insurance agency, asked me if I wanted to work in insurance sales. I realized that my life would not be in danger, or at least I thought not. Of course, when I found out what people thought of insurance salesmen, I wasn't quite so sure I was out of harm's way. However, I thought this sounded like a pretty good deal. I could sell insurance and make commission. I decided to try it and sell insurance policies door to door.

I promised myself then, as long as I worked in insurance or any other field, as I moved up the corporate ranks, I would never belittle a colleague or have a fellow employee serve me because they worked at a lower level.

This philosophy was taught to me a long time ago by my very first boss, Alexander Cortezzo, who I worked for at age fifteen. One day when I was preparing to leave for college, he told me to **remember all the people I had passed on the way up the ladder because they would be the same I pass on the way down.** I never forgot that man and I think about him often because the lessons he taught me were more important than any professor or business partner I have ever had.

He also taught me a lesson in creating reality. He had a small soda distributorship. On Mondays, I would work on the soda truck delivering to his customers. His larger competitors could not understand how he could occupy so much shelf space when his products were much higher priced than anyone else's. What they failed to witness was the "Cortezzo Factor". He would spend hours at those stores, talking to the owners, and helping them with little projects. I would do odd jobs in the stores for the owners while they sat and talked with Cortezzo. I would even do repairs or maybe move an item that was too heavy for the owner to lift. I witnessed customer service by watching him. I learned it was about people caring about people; it wasn't about a job title.

Recently, I ran out of business cards. I asked the person who orders our supplies to order my business cards without any title because titles mean nothing in the world in which we play. I learned from that old man the skill and the style of treating customers like friends and trying to deliver the best you could to meet their needs. I never worry about whether or not the proper term is client or customer. For me the proper label is friend. It sure makes the delivery of service much easier.

After being in insurance sales for two years, I was fortunate to become manager of one of the branch offices. Working in a small town for a small company, I had exposure to all different aspects of the business, everything from sales to management. I was excited because I had gone from the construction site and bill collection to professional sales. Along the way I learned that reputation is everything.

Once my daughter, Tara, and I were in a K-Mart and as we turned the corner we faced an individual who I had chased for collections. After we recognized each other, he immediately dropped all his items on the floor and sprinted out of K-Mart. It was difficult to explain to a ten-year old why people were looking at her dad and running wildly from the store.

The reputations we build in business or in our social life are critical.

That was one reputation I didn't appreciate having, but it was certainly effective in my work as a bill collector.

One of my favorite moments of creating reality was with my sales people. During a meeting break, I arranged to have a make-up artist waiting for me in my office. During a fifteen minute break he proceeded to make me look ancient. He took his make-up and worked on my face and my eyes. He sprayed my hair to gray it, and drew wrinkles in my face with a pencil liner. He worked his magic in six minutes and I gave the illusion of a man in his late seventies. It was amazing what this guy did to me. Just by following the lines that I have now, and accentuating them, he made me an old man. Scary stuff when you realize how little time you actually have to make a difference.

The break now over, I walked back into the room. People didn't notice right away, but as I approached the boardroom table, Dave, one of my colleagues said, "Oh man, Anthony must have got bad news. Somebody must have died or something." I started to speak to my sales people as though it were the future and they were gone, retired or deceased. Therefore, if Bob had a daughter, Morgan, I talked to him as though he was Morgan. I proceeded to talk to each one of them as if I were speaking to their children. I told each one of them about his mother or father and what a difference they had made in my life as I prepared for retirement. My sales people became filled with emotion and they cried about something called "reality". In minutes, with a little make-up, I was able to create the reality of the future.

As leaders what we want to have happen is to try to be as good as our children think we are.

That's the trick. Your children think you are wonderful. Even when you make mistakes, they want you to come back and be wonderful. It's important that you are their role model. If we all strive to be as good as our children think we are, we will be at a level to reach out and pull our children to a level of their own reality.

II

THE STONE CUTTER

II

THE STONE CUTTER

I believe people are born with a primary skill package. Our primary skill package is a supply of endurance, strength, flexibility and skill. Just as there are some athletes who don't have to train hard and can excel in certain sports, I believe there are certain people who, without training, have a skill package that they bring to the game of life. We have the responsibility to take the same four items – endurance, strength, flexibility and skill and expand upon those items throughout life.

One of the first lessons I ever learned about the primary skill package was by watching Alexander Cortezzo. He would explain to me how people had abilities that came without trying. He was a self-made man who owned a swimming pool, a grove, a campground and a little soda business. The jobs he gave me exposed me to different kinds of work from construction skills to lifeguarding. One day he tried to teach me how to cut stone. He showed me that I had the basic skills of a laborer. Through being able to push a wheelbarrow uphill, load it with fieldstone and push it back down, I realized these skills were a form of a primary package.

However cutting the stone was a totally different issue. He would lift a stone up on his leg, hit it with a hammer and cut it like scissors to paper. I hit it with a hammer and it shattered into pieces. I remember years later, he gave that very stone hammer to me with a piece of paper rubber banded to the handle that said, "When you learn to use this hammer, you'll be an artist and you'll be a man." Though I never learned to cut stone like he did, I never forgot the lessons that old man taught me. I learned later that the stone hammer was from his father. The rock we cut together is part of the fireplace in my parent's home. Rocks like Cortezzo have a way of securing our walls if we let them chisel our package.

It was also Alexander Cortezzo, not some textbook or counselor who taught me how to manage stress and learn the art of relaxation. In April and May when we would be working like dogs at the bottom of a cement pool trying to prepare for the summer season, I noticed he would often sit under the same oak tree. One day at lunch time he yelled down to me, "Hey, Squirrel come up here." The reason why I was called Squirrel was because I had amazed him once by shimmying up a flag pole and painting it on the way down. When I asked him what he wanted, he asked that I come up there and talk to his tree. I declined, finding it hard enough to talk to girls let alone talk to trees. He said again, "Come up here and talk to this tree." All he would do was lay under that tree and look up into its branches. He really would speak to that tree as if it were a friend, usually questioning it about life. It took years working there before I could tell you that on certain days I spoke to that damn tree. He was teaching me that humanity and nature are linked and that the basis of stress reduction and relaxation was to be able to communicate with ourselves through nature.

The conversations that we have with people are so limited, "Hi, how are you?" "Fine, how are you?". We never really engage each other. Even husbands and wives rarely take the opportunity to discuss what is truly important. Everyone you speak to in the workplace is busy, but how many are productive? How many take the time to speak to themselves and to others and reflect on where they are going.

It's no longer enough to be busy; you must be productive, animated and energetic in every task you try to accomplish.

I remember asking my father after his retirement from Bethlehem Steel, if he could remember what issue in managing men caused him the most stress. He couldn't remember. This was a man with a mind like a steel trap, but he could not remember. If you asked me today what have been the most stressful experiences in my business career, I certainly could tell you. Men like Mr. Cortezzo and my dad forever paint life's canvas through their artistry. They focused on the future and not the past. In 1997, a friend of the family found my dad's hard hat in the pipe shop of Bethlehem Steel. The shop was scheduled to be demolished, but now his hard hat rests safely in my office. Champions always find a new shop to work in because time has a way to continue for these great people long after they are gone.

III

THE PINNACLE OF GREATNESS

III

THE PINNACLE OF GREATNESS

I n 1977, my dad found out that he would need bypass heart surgery. Not once during his recovery period did I ever hear my father complain about pain or discomfort. As a matter of fact, as a young boy I never remember my father complaining about anything. I never remember my father having a harsh word to say about anyone. Years later, after fully recovering from heart surgery, my dad was diagnosed with cancer. For years he battled through every treatment, from radiation to chemotherapy to experimental drugs. Never once did I hear my father complain. There were times when he was frustrated by the slow recovery or depressed by the diagnosis of having cancer, but every day he treated the cancer as though it were a common cold and continued on with his life.

After battling cancer, he was then diagnosed with Lou Gehrig's Disease. Those who are familiar with this terrible illness, know that it is debilitating and cruel. Finally on November 21, 1995, my dad passed away. Not only did he have Lou Gehrig's Disease, but he had a cancerous tumor in his stomach area which prevented him from taking what little nourishment we could offer him after LGD left him with an inability to swallow food or liquid. Never once during this terrible illness did I hear my father complain.

When remembering my dad, I am often embarrassed and ashamed that I complain about minimal issues or speak ill of others. He was fortunate to have his wish, which was to pass away in his home with the family he so loved. We were very fortunate to be able to care for this great man. The lessons he taught the family will be remembered throughout our lives. When I lost my dad, I lost a great friend and mentor. Rarely, when I was growing up and trying to excel in the business world, did I think to ask my father for his opinion. It wasn't until I became older that I realized that this man who had no plaques, trophies or testimonials hanging in his house, was probably the best source of motivation and mentorship.

So what place does this story of my dad have to do with business, motivation and success? I believe that Dad exemplified success. It wasn't about money. Dad showed that success wasn't about money, material items, or titles on business cards. It's not about cars and homes because, in the end, those things become the possessions of others or testimonials to a hollow existence. My dad, a welder by trade (not formally educated), an athlete, an artist, a writer and a man of the family, truly defined success. So, I believe the pinnacle of success, that pinnacle of greatness we all strive to achieve, is the fact that when our final days come, there is someone who will try to model what we did or be like who we were. As I mentioned before, the challenge is to be as good as our children think we are, and that was my father. He truly was as good as my sister, Phyllis, and I thought. He had this ability to bring happiness and joy to everyone who knew him. Today, and for years to come, many of us will try to model ourselves after my father. What better definition of success than that. My father, the welder, still molds our steel.

The pinnacle of greatness comes from regeneration, that as we achieve, others will seek to achieve and surpass us.

This is why it is so critical that we surround ourselves with people who are better than we are. They can take our marks of achievement to the next level. I believe the core of business and negotiation is encased in these issues. People who are out solely for their own benefit will never be truly successful and never attain the pinnacle of greatness. We must blaze a trail for others to follow.

Dad was also the best definition I have seen for the embodiment of stress management. We have what I refer to as "stress of the day"; trendy continual issues of discussing stress only in a very clinical and scientific way. Everything from diet to exercise are important, but all are terminal. We all know that there are going to be days when we don't exercise enough. Maybe we won't eat right for months or years. What I learned from my dad and others like him is that the true management of stress is to push ourselves everyday to the limit of our ability. I am talking about men and women doing the best they can every day. I believe that with stress comes the ability to grow. Just like the body develops a callus in the areas that it uses the most, I believe that our mental state develops in the same way. The more we achieve, the more protective callus we build on our mental attitude.

My father was challenged by many different illnesses. There are many people who are faced with one death issue and quit. But Dad was a man who had heart disease, cancer and Lou Gehrig's Disease, who eventually starved to death, and never complained. Is it really so tough for us to look past our little challenges? To be caught in those petty problems is to insult the suffering of the strong.

IV

MISSION POSSIBLE

IV

MISSION POSSIBLE

I have a simple mission statement that states my desire *to be a welcomed leader in any arena I choose to stand.* We need to think about our goals, direction, focus, and stick with them. Your mission statement is not about your job. Where people make mistakes is that they build their life and their identity around a job, a spouse or family. Our mission and vision statements allow us to conduct ourselves as our own business.

Just like organizations do SWOT Analyses (strengths, weaknesses, opportunities and threats), it is just as vital to the success of individuals and leaders to do SWOT Analyses on themselves. How many of us really look at our strengths, weaknesses, opportunities and threats? How many of us really build a personal mission statement and a personal vision statement and stick to it? I have asked our sales force to do that very thing. I have asked students in my classroom to do that very thing. Many of them view this as an assignment, do it, and never use it again. How many of you in your organizations have people right under your nose who are recognized outside their organizations as leaders in their fields and you fail to capitalize on it? You failed to tap the oil that is lying right under your own ground. You can blend your colleagues' mission statements together and form a set of by-laws to guide your collective cultures to success.

We have to set a strategy and a mission statement, for ourselves, both short and long term, that keeps us focused on the tasks and challenges that lie ahead.

V

PERSONAL DYNAMIC MARKETING PLAN

V

PERSONAL DYNAMIC MARKETING PLAN

E ach person needs to have a personal marketing plan that profiles their strengths, and makes them visible to those around them. Just like we use résumés to secure positions in our careers, we must have a personal marketing plan that helps define our personal delivery system.

A personal marketing plan is one that incorporates formal education, goal development and risk taking. It defines our patterns of whether we are successful on completing tasks and whether or not we have the ability to be creative. I believe that many of our national politicians lack a personal dynamic marketing plan. What they pursue is a public relations plan and the marketing of issues or attacking their opponent. They fail, however, to show their personal visions in personal marketing plan deliveries. If our politicians and professionals concentrated more on vision than the technique of the day or the trend of the times, they would be more successful in retaining their offices.

Leonard Gruppo has served in the PA state legislature for what is becoming his tenth term. He has been successfully reelected over the last eighteen years and is beginning to serve his nineteenth and twentieth years. In all the years of his campaigning, never once did he negatively campaign against an opponent; yet, time after time his opponents have negatively campaigned against him. I remember his very first campaign eighteen years ago. As a very young politician he was being mentored by the party and prior candidates who had lost in several prior elections to the incumbent. The political pundits suggested to Len that he campaign on the negative issues of his opponent. He flatly refused to do that and, in fact, some people left his camp. He would spend countless hours after work going door to door in his districts. He is someone who has a personal dynamic marketing plan. He is always campaigning. He doesn't wait until 120 days before the election and stick a ton of campaign signs in the ground; he is out there every day campaigning through good service to his constituents. His personal dynamic marketing plan is to serve the needs of his constituents, deliver good service and never act in a negative way against an opponent. What I have found fascinating is that term after term, rarely does an opponent call and congratulate him. I think that speaks volumes of the type of opponents he faced versus how he conducted his own campaign.

There are people like my cousin, Len Gruppo, all around us. These are the people we need to model ourselves after and seek out to help us implement our own personal dynamic marketing plans.

VI

DREAM RIDERS

VI

DREAM RIDERS

W hat has happened is we have stopped riding our dreams. When do you last remember dreaming about your future? Let's go back to the earliest time we can remember dreaming as children. Is it so difficult to dream as an adult? Those with dreams and visions create reality for ourselves and others. When we fail to dream, our focus becomes the routine. You must be able to focus your subconscious, visualize your dream and seek to obtain it.

**You don't pursue money, you pursue your dreams,
and then they pay you for it. It's that simple.**

If you can still dream, start thinking of yourselves as businesses. What I would like you to think about is never having to work for someone again. The most successful people I know, even though they are an employee somewhere, never really think of themselves as working for someone.

They always think of themselves as being self-employed. I want you to start thinking like that. It is not easy because people always want you to believe that it's not possible. It is possible because often others become passengers on our dream. Remember, dream riders are necessary to make the dream reality.

VII

PERSONAL BOARD OF DIRECTORS

VII

PERSONAL BOARD OF DIRECTORS

L et's call ourselves Dreamer Enterprises. Imagine you are the President and you have total ownership of your company. Start to recruit families or support people to become managers of your company. When we talk about creating reality, one of the first things that we have to determine and understand for ourselves is that we function as our own company and as our own entity. If, for example, we refer to our company as Dreamer Enterprise, Inc., we would visualize ourselves at the top of the organizational structure with total ownership over achievements and endeavors that we try to accomplish. Under that structure exist positions for family, friends, and co-workers who serve as assistants to our Dreamer Enterprises. Your colleagues, people you work with, friends and co-workers, are in place to support your organization. They are your employees. This will look a lot different than what you know to be the corporate structure of most companies, but it is a healthy way to look at it. I love to see organizational charts, the Presidents, the Vice Presidents. What nonsense! The chart is there for the structure of your organization, but is not a motivation to the people. How can you possibly motivate somebody if you show them an organizational chart and they are three rows from the top. It's an immediate demotivator. Just by seeing their name so low makes it harder for them to dream. Religious groups, professionals and volunteers all become employees of your company.

One of the items I want to stress is that if you are your own company, I believe that it is critical that you form your own board of directors. You are the CEO of your company, and you need a board to advise you. No matter where you go, no matter where you work, no matter who you lead or manage, or how many companies you own, you will have a jump because your system of personal management is portable, flexible and staffed with quality board members.

One of the prerequisites that we look at when we form a personal Board of Directors is the fact that we want people to be winners and compatible partners that bring diversified backgrounds with the ability to meet and match up with our culture and deliver the creation of our reality.

We want the personal Board of Directors to challenge us and to help us create. We have to think of ourselves as creators. Not only do we create an environment and a reality for ourselves, but it also becomes very contagious to those around us. It is important when interviewing our personal Board of Directors we select people who enable us to be creators, allowing us to be challenged. We need directors who won't let us take an easy road in running our own company. You do not want to stand with those who constantly underachieve. Your parents do not want you to, your friends don't want you to and I don't want you to. If you have them in your life now and they have the ability to manipulate you, you need to neutralize them.

You only want to stand with winners. A personal Board of Directors, composed of winners, make compatible partners. These are people who can challenge you to be better than you are, who won't give you the yes answers, but aren't totally different than you. You do not want to include somebody so totally out of your network of thinking, who can make the cure worse than the disease. You want to make sure they are compatible with you.

It could be anyone that you would like to have as a partner. They must be able to mentally challenge you. How do you know when you are being challenged? These people make you think outside your box. They will not permit you to remain locked inside a mental comfort zone. Our personal Board of Directors continues to kick our box until the sides collapse and creativity flows free.

You want to associate with creators; you do not want human lint. You want people who create their own destiny and create their own reality.

They are the ones you want around you, that can create in you something different. They can make you think of yourself differently and project you to a new level of achievement.

VIII

YOUR OPPOSITE HAND

VIII

YOUR OPPOSITE HAND

D id you ever try to sign your name with your opposite hand and notice how long it takes and that it rarely looks like your dominant hand's signature? In fact, it is difficult to hold the pen properly. Yet, think of all the skills we can do with both of our hands that allow us to function in life's everyday situations. I think it would be interesting to make a contract with ourselves to hire a personal Board of Directors by including the development of a personal dynamic marketing plan and a mission and vision statement. We must attempt to possess an optimistic attitude that improves the morale of others and helps those less fortunate than ourselves; that is, produce a contract and sign it with our opposite hand. Realizing how difficult it is to sign our name with our opposite hand is a visualization of how difficult it is for the human being to excel at all the choices and expectations we face. There are no loopholes in a contract with ourselves.

The more capable and confident we become at difficult tasks, the closer we come to our achievement of the pinnacle of greatness.

And what a struggle it is every day to stay on track with a contract we make with ourselves. So why not take a moment to jot down three areas of self development to focus on and then sign our name with our opposite hand? Your future is waiting, so go ahead and sign the agreement and begin to deliver on your dreams.

IX

FAITH

IX

FAITH

I nspiration comes from all the people with which we interact. We must have faith in the human spirit and be open to allow people to access our vision.

People we least expect may become a guide to our future. Look around – are your best advisors in your profession? I sincerely doubt the answer to be yes. If it is, you may be short arming your opportunities and vision.

It is foolish for us, as professionals, to only surround ourselves with those who can further our careers or improve our profiles in business models. I once asked my college students, if I blindfolded someone and put a sports trophy in their hands, would they be able to describe what it was. What we knew to be true was the person would probably be able to identify it as a trophy, made out of metal or wood, with a man or woman with their arms outstretched against the frame very much like we would define a crucifix. I believe that if I put a crucifix in a blindfolded person's hand, he would certainly be able to identify it because the cross is a universal symbol. I believe, as does Jim Rogers, head of Sports Medicine at Temple

University, from whom I first learned of this type of concept, at sporting events we should give children crucifixes instead of trophies. Because I believe that the greatest source of inspiration which gives us the ability to achieve is our faith – a faith in God and a faith in ourselves. It was my dad's faith in God, himself and his family that kept him strong in the end. As the time came closer, not knowing on what night his life would end, he spoke to his family members with kind words and encouragement, desperately hoping he would be remembered as someone who loved them. *Dad, if you can hear me now – mission accomplished.*

X

FEAR – THE TOTAL OF LOST MOMENTS

X

FEAR – THE TOTAL OF LOST MOMENTS

My definition of fear is the total of lost moments.

As we look back over our lives and take a hard look at the areas where we have been successful or unsuccessful, it is interesting to find that many times it's fear that has prevented us from achieving our goals and creating a healthy reality for ourselves and those around us. It is the fear we face when we go back and look over what we have accomplished and find, perhaps, what we have created can be taken from us at any moment. We tend toward complacency and fall into that personal comfort zone which has a deadly impact on us as individuals, our employers and those around us.

There are six areas I feel are critical in dealing with our fears and moving on.

The first one is **confidence**. The way to feel confident is to know that everyone has fear. Everyone, even the most successful individual, has had his moments of fear. **We need to know that the only failure is in not trying anything new.**

We have to **trust** in ourselves that we can accomplish new horizons and we can stay focused on the task at hand.

It is important that we be **honest** with ourselves. We must admit when we have weaknesses instead of trying to hide them, strive to identify them, work with them and move forward.

A **knowledge** of ourselves is necessary to understand how we will react in all our endeavors. Then failure is a learning experience and becomes a future motivator.

Look for the **courage** it takes to continue to push forward and stay focused when the tide is against us.

Finally, of course, is **drive**. Drive is a very misunderstood word. It is a concept that forces us everyday to continue to **work harder and harder.**

Fear comes in different containers. It is the absence of fear that brings us to the doorstep of comfort. When we reach this doorstep, we choose to enter or return and confront our fears.

Everyone eventually reaches the level of belief that he has mastered his personality and abilities, but, in reality, it is a focus that allows routine and presents the illusion of success. But we, as individuals, understand how critical it is to confront our fears so we can move forward. I refer to it as a point of "reaching our doorstep". That's where we come to the point where we have tried our best, but now face new hurdles and obstacles. We must take a moment, take a breath, turn and look at these fears, confront them, master them and move on. There is a secret to success, and that secret comes in establishing a winning environment. It was once said that it is important we not waste time judging others, but focus on our own tasks and what we have to do to succeed. We have to obtain commitment, not only from those around us, but from ourselves. We must strive to outdistance our former selves.

It is always interesting to me when we look at photographs of ourselves from small children to present day, the one thing that never lies, the one thing that shows an accurate picture is our eyes. If we truly look at the eyes of the child and ask ourselves, "Although the container has changed

53

around us, is there still a fire – is there still a furnace that burns inside that physical container that we can see through our eyes?" So whether we stand in front of a mirror and look at our eyes, do it through a photograph, through the eyes of our own children, other family members, or our personal Board of Directors, it is important we determine if the fire is still there. If it isn't, we need to ignite it.

It is important to obtain a commitment from ourselves and those around us that we will strive with others to obtain our goals.

It is important to select objectives and work in small components. Sometimes we form a scheme that is too grandiose and that makes it difficult to achieve success and stay focused. We need to inform ourselves of what we are trying to accomplish and take a realistic look at how our progress is going. Volunteer for the tough project. We will find, after taking on a project, albeit a tough one, we were the ones who volunteered for it and we're out there alone. We have the ability to succeed where others haven't. The major issue is to succeed where we haven't, to find a new level to raise the bar to-higher than we imagine possible.

Isolation is the privilege to experiment with new visions.

It is important that we clearly articulate our fears – look at what our underlying fear is and try to deal with it on a day-to-day basis. We need to look for the origins of our fear. Is our fear from a long term struggle or the result of internal or external pressure? It is important that we make an active decision about our direction. If we find ourselves stumbling and find it difficult to continue, we need to stop and evaluate our position before we move on. We can obtain support and encouragement by talking to others about our fears and concerns.

XI

RAINMAKERS

XI

RAINMAKERS

D uring our lives we all face people I refer to as "rainmakers". These are people without ambition and goals who tend to feel defeated and often deliver empty promises. Although we all come in contact with these underachieving individuals, it is important that we recognize them and do our best to stay focused and on track. Many times we can have a positive effect on a rainmaker. I have observed situations where someone who has a negative attitude and a pessimistic outlook, is turned around by surrounding himself with winners.

**Hopefully you can serve on the personal Board of
Directors to those individuals who are looking
for the rain instead of the sunshine.**

Do you think there are people who want to see you fail? The more successful you become, the more powerful you become. Why would someone want to see you fail? Jealousy? Others, with low expectations of themselves, have to weigh themselves against you. The more successful you are, the harder it becomes for them.

The following are symptoms of a sick professional:

- Do you blame others for your failures?

- Do you envy the success of colleagues?

- Are you rewriting your list after a few items?

- Do you have more than one stack of files on your desk?

- Is your desk top free of debris at the end of the day?

- Do you believe if you handle a situation, from beginning to end, the result will be more successful?

- Do you constantly ask more than one colleague's opinion on an issue you are trying to resolve?

- Do you have three separate organizational systems in your office or your home?

- Do you pick up a file and return it without accomplishing a task?

- Do you work best right before a deadline?

- Do you often divert from a project problem to work on another separate issue?

- Do you have discussions to convince yourself that you are doing the proper amount of work in your job?

At one time or another, we are all patients with these symptoms. We must continue to seek treatment because everyone wants us in perfect leadership health. Eventually, you become the antidote for another's illnesses.

XII

THE NON-PROFIT PROFESSIONAL

XII

THE NON-PROFIT PROFESSIONAL

I discussed the need to surround ourselves with personal Boards of Directors that are compatible to us. Sometimes I think we look too far for these people when they are often right under our nose.

One of the finest professionals I have had the honor to work with over the years is the President of a large behavioral health company in Lancaster, Pennsylvania. This woman purchased an agency and turned it from a small regional company into one that is recognized around the country for successful services to behavioral healthcare clients. I have had the good fortune to spend time with her and her leadership team and I have watched these people accomplish very difficult challenges. She, like many other professionals in her field, always believes she is not equipped to do battle in the business arena. I have found her to be well-armed, capable and powerful because she brings to the table what few business people possess – concern for the client. I once heard her say in a speech, "**You can take care of business by taking care of people.**" These health care professionals have no hidden agenda. Personal opportunity is not at the top of their list. There is no bravado, it is not ego driven at the expense of

65

others. Their driving force is a kind and caring manner that allows them to succeed.

Most often in the for-profit business world, we know something isn't exactly right, but we proceed as we have been because it is difficult to change. I have witnessed in the non-profit sector leaders, parents, teachers and counselors helping the system change so decisions made will not mean the elimination of services for their clients. In the business world, others joke that social workers do not make good business people. I believe the opposite to be true. I believe that business people could stand a bit of social worker in their portfolios of professionalism.

The issues that affect our lives and the lives of those we love have the most impact on us. I will never forget after Dad passed away, the outpouring of support I received from the non-profit community. Men and women all over the country sent the most beautiful cards, letters and symbols of affection to me and my family during our time of loss. It is a level of greatness. That is their level of greatness that these professionals leave to the world. I want to be like them. When my friends and colleagues have lost family, I try to conduct myself according to the standards of the non-profit professional. They always find time in their schedules to care for a friend. Yet every day, I see them struggle to run their businesses better, to be able to raise money and confront other important hurdles to stay in operation. They have already achieved greatness in the eyes of people who have successful businesses, power and money. **They have what few possess – the ability to engage the human spirit**. If there is anything in this book that I would share with you as far as marketing and motivation, it would be the inspiration that professionals like them create for the entire world community.

In 1986, I decided to spearhead a project for our company to begin to serve providers in the non-profit arena. It was a different world for me when I first started working with them. These people were kind and compassionate, they were into analysis and processing of issues – large and small. They were people who were paid salaries much too low for their ability and the magnitude of the job; yet every day they fought to help others.

For most of us, success is defined by wealth and power, yet these professionals define success by those they serve. While the non-profit sector is always trying to run like the for-profit sector and be more business-minded, I think they have more to teach than they have to learn. I think if we could all incorporate their values into our day-to-day workplaces, the arena in which we play would be better off.

I developed a theory in a seminar called "For Prophet For Today". **I believe the key to being a better person is the ability to create a prophecy for yourself and those you work with.** In my seminar "For Prophet For Today", I speak about the need to develop an organizational prophecy. As time passes, we realize that whether we are for-profit or non-profit we must create a personal and organizational prophecy driven by the desire to help others.

XIII

HONOR THE HUMANITY

XIII

HONOR THE HUMANITY

I had the extreme good fortune to be able to have dinner in September of 1996 with Cardinal Joseph Bernadin from Chicago. Being in Cardinal Bernadin's presence for a few moments made you realize that you were in the presence of a very humble, kind and wonderful man. At the time I had the opportunity to meet him, he was suffering from cancer which within two months, would take his life. He spoke that evening on the rights of children and the need to dedicate a portion of ourselves to serving those who are less fortunate. Had our organization not become involved in the non-profit arena, I would have missed the opportunities to meet people like Cardinal Bernadin who have an impact not only on our own lives, but on the lives of others.

Leaders don't just lead in the workplace. Leaders lead and create reality for everyone they meet regardless of the environment. I was reminded of this in a very direct way on November 20, 1996. My friend Bob's father, Jack, had just passed away within a few days of the first anniversary of my dad's death. When my father died, I felt it was important to speak about him during the funeral, so I wrote and delivered his eulogy entitled,

71

"Always the Soldier". During his father's funeral, Bob rose and felt it was important to speak about his dad. Emotionally, it was very difficult for me that day. It was only one day until the anniversary of my father's death. I was captivated by Bob's words and it brought a comfort to me for the feelings I knew I would have the next day. I realized that leaders and leadership are connected to family and integrity and honor and valor more than I think many of us care to admit.

Business textbooks rarely address the emotional issues of leadership and management which come directly from courage and heart and the ability to remember those who have led before us.

I think as managers, motivators, parents and leaders, we have to observe the events which happen to the people around us. We have to use our experiences to support them during their crises. We have to rise above traditional management techniques and look to help colleagues with the social and emotional issues which impact them at home and in the workplace. The loss of loved ones, divorce, troubled children and failure at the achievements they are trying to accomplish all have an impact on our colleagues. It is our responsibility, as we create reality for ourselves and our corporations, to be sensitive to creating positive reality for those we work with. If we have lost loved ones, when that unfortunate turn happens to our colleagues it is our responsibility to help them through those moments of grief. Let them know we went through it, then guide and comfort them with our experiences.

Often we tend only to concentrate on the processes and results of our life. We must seek to honor all humanity through the power of achievement strapped to the body of good will and the strength that comes from engaging life's challenges.

XIV

THE DONATION OF MOTIVATION

XIV

THE DONATION OF MOTIVATION

Concentrate less on the financial rewards of business and become a motivational donor.

What if I was to tell you most people think money is a motivator? Would you agree with me? I will tell you in the beginning I thought it was, but the older and more experienced I became, I realized it can't be. Because if it was, then why would people in the non-profit field be so highly motivated to care for other human beings? What drives is not the money. It's a vision and the visualization of success. We have moved away from dream-based management and we lack visualization.

We should all visualize our future. Perhaps it is to own our own business, be in charge of organizations, manage regional operations or go international. If you visualize that picture now and put it in your head, you will get there, and the money will come. Making money, that's easy. It's not the hard part of the game. If you are a hard worker, (which most people aren't), if you are not complacent (most people are) and if you can get out of your own way and generate enough horsepower to pass yourself, you will make plenty of money. However, you may not be motivated to continue through the difficult stages. The following are areas of motivation to guide you when the motivational road is under construction:

Perception. The perception is that we motivate ourselves. It is common thinking. If you want to stay motivated, get in a situation where you can help people less fortunate and feel better about yourself.

Resources. You can't motivate your colleagues or your superiors if they do not have the resources. If people aren't being paid a salary that meets their basic needs, it's very difficult to motivate them. You have to give them the resources in order for them to be equal in the game.

Training. The best type of training that you can give a person is to get them involved in real scenarios. There are people who have worked in companies many years without being subjected to actual business scenarios. They constantly are protected from action and deal only in the routine. When we need their assistance later, they are intimidated to enter the battle.

Motivation begins with **cross-training**. You must cross-train to get a taste of the difficult parts of the business. I encourage you to try your best to sample some difficult areas. We all need an appreciation of our co-workers' challenges.

Aptitude. There are some people, no matter how motivated, who just do not have the aptitude for the job. Some people are just never going to go beyond where they are. However, their stability can be the foundation for future growth.

In my experience, motivation is the knowledge of ourselves and how we will react in certain scenarios. The more we focus and understand our behavior, the easier for us to reach new levels of achievement.

Critical in motivation is the expectations of others. Do not expect from your people what you can't expect from yourself. I am not talking about ability, I am talking about attitude, about drive and determination. There are people you will surround yourself with who will be better than you. Never fear them surpassing you. That will demotivate you and force you to hold them in check.

Surround yourself with people who are better than you and encourage them to succeed.

You have to drive yourself harder than they do. What you are looking for are the people who are impact players. In every division, in every area of the company, you are looking for people who are able to be promoted and become motivated to excel at certain levels. You give them the most training and encouragement. They are the ones who achieve higher levels and assist those around them. Don't expect to reach everyone. By developing a system of winners you will elevate everyone's performance. There are ways to motivate by your own example. If your workers are working on a Saturday, you have to be there. If your people are working overtime, don't bother them, but be there and be visible.

Incentives. There have been many books written on creative incentive programs. Ask people how they are motivated by incentives. Is it trips, bonuses? You want the incentive plan to be long-term. If you made a goal you thought was a challenge in a given year, don't fall into the trap of making the next goal unattainable. Be sure they receive a dose of success. Changing their goals every year because they have accomplished them is not appropriate behavior as a leader. If the goal was too easy then it could serve as a demotivator.

Personal discussions are still one of the best ways to recognize a job well done. Your colleagues like to hear praise directly from you. They like to see your face and hear your voice. For example, broadcast it on the office voicemail. You can broadcast in a minute to all the workers. I get on the voicemail and announce, " I want to take a moment to congratulate Brian for a tremendous job he did on the project we worked on in Michigan. Because of his hard work, we were very successful in landing a client." Now, that's all it took. Hit one button and the message goes to all the employees. I always end with, "Please join me in congratulating Brian for a job well done." When I started doing this years ago, what percentage of people do you think got up and went to see Brian or left him a message or sent him a memo? The concept was new so I believe the percentage was high. But as time progressed, the percentage dropped because recognition became routine.

As leaders we must attempt to motivate all employees. Do we have channels available to monitor the successes of our colleagues? Do we neglect their accomplishments if the achievement is not important to our goals? Do we try to "top" their achievements with our own? Whether it is our children or our colleagues, we must recognize their achievements, great or small.

The recognition of colleagues is a leader's major role. One Christmas I sent a letter to the children of the sales team members. I wrote in the letter my appreciation for their parents' accomplishments. I expressed my pride in their parents or loved one. I placed a gift certificate for a restaurant in with the letter that said, "You can take Mom and Dad out to dinner for Christmas with this." These small gestures lift a person high. Remember, never have a system in place that beats them up to the same degree it rewards them.

The recognition of success must always be greater than the discussion of failure.

XV

ATTACK

XV

ATTACK

I love hand stamps. Don't you just love the traditional ones like CONFIDENTIAL, SECOND REQUEST, FILE, URGENT, PAST DUE? I feel we should design our own stamp that helps us with motivation, one that sends a clear message to people around us. My hand stamp has letters about one inch high and simply says, "ATTACK". I stamp the word "ATTACK" in red ink on certain projects when I want people to have a major concentration and focus. I use the word "ATTACK" because I want people to attack the challenge. I want them to attack the project and realize that the request goes well beyond urgent or second notice; it places a descriptor on the situation in a context that needs no further explanation on my part.

In dedication, every warrior has a mission. Every warrior can state a purpose, but only the warrior left standing had a dedication.

The day I wrote that was the day I lost a major deal; I remember having everything perfect. I had this great mission, the perfect purpose. I had a purpose for which saints are martyred. I couldn't believe anything could go wrong, but it did because I was never dedicated to it. I was merely a delivery boy. That is not dedication. Dedication crushes all obstacles.

Unless you have dedication, you are not going to make it. I'll never forget my blue collar past. Those workers had a blue collar dedication and passion. I never see my shirt collar as white because under every color of work shirt is the sweat that gives a drink to our dreams.

We need a time card machine to deliver the message. I bought a year's supply of time cards and handed them to my sales people and encouraged them to envision an internal time clock. When I say punching the clock, I mean start a process or start a goal. I don't care when you finish it, if you are fast or slow, have energy or lack energy, just start doing something. Then you can only punch out when the job is done. Imagine if corporate America was paid on a piece rate system, based on how many pieces of success you have in a day.

The blue collar world provides a better "tired" at the end of the day than the white collar world. The body is worked and then it rests. Often in the corporate world we cheat on our "tired" because we fail to work our minds. We prevent the good form of "tired" and we never rest well. We must punch the clock and deliver all our body weight to the movement of the task.

**We can remove any stain of spilled failure if we
scrub it out with a circular motion of dedication
and blue collar work ethic.**

While conducting a motivational meeting, I wore construction work gloves on my hands. I illustrated the need for corporate professionals to have blue collar structure. During the session, I removed the work gloves to display a pair of surgical gloves underneath. I focused on the need for professionals to not only attack the "construction" of our goals, but to "operate" on our skills and personality. We must never miss the details and the delicate balance of our path to achievement.

**Achievement allows us to be two people. One is at
work on the goal and the other fine tunes the
internal machinery.**

XVI

CORPORATE JUVENILE DELINQUENTS

XVI

CORPORATE JUVENILE DELINQUENTS

Wouldn't we rather be surrounded by corporate juvenile delinquents than people who function in the box and fail to motivate themselves, producing a negative influence on those around them?

I feel there should be a little bit of corporate juvenile delinquency in all of us, and God knows I have made my contribution over the years. It is the corporate delinquent who seeks a better path to the delivery of goals.

Every day we have to act like it is our first day on the job. We have to show our true texture, the true quality of ourselves as valuable people in the world.

For my college students, I conducted a final exam on what I termed hand-to-hand combat. I placed a management scenario for each student to draw at random from a box. They had ten minutes to resolve the problem.

I refer to these as the "Toughies". They are the toughest questions and scenarios we can face as professionals. Every day, we need to think as juvenile delinquents. Every day, we need to think and act like we are in hand-to-hand combat. We must vow not to take any decision lightly and look for the techniques and advantages that help us with our reputation, routine and our reality. I think that these issues help us build attitude. I think it helps us from sliding from positive attitudes to the negative. It gives us that stability, that staying power to hold our attitudes at the appropriate level for longer periods of time.

People with positive attitudes learn how to question achievement.

We need to know how people in our lives win or lose. What I mean by this is, when do they feel successful? When do they feel as though they have won in a particular battle, because there are different levels of winning and losing? Some people may feel they don't truly lose until they are physically removed from a situation. For others the mere smirk or tone of a voice can make them feel lost or beaten. We have to discover the previously unidentified issues that affect people. As I mentioned before, what have life's experiences done to them? I am always amazed, as I am sure you are, that there are entire families that have negative thinking generation after generation. That no matter what you say to them, they will find a negative response to it. Why did this occur? What life experiences were forced upon them? What failure in the mentor process occurred that created negative thinking generation after generation? If the initial generation was never rewarded or praised, chances are that the system continued from child to child, parent to parent.

Previously, I talked about your personal Board of Directors. It is critical to surround yourself with winners. Yet, if our colleagues or we, ourselves, come from negative thinking families or negative thinking environments, how are we to even know a winner? We have no qualifications, we bring no skills to locating winners. In fact, people who are known to be winners, could become offensive to the negative thinker. They could impact them in a less positive manner. That is why we often struggle in business with pessimists, when in reality they have known no other system. How could we expect them to surround themselves with winners when that is the farthest person from their knowledge base? It is important, then, for us to know our own work habits. What causes us to lose a positive attitude edge? What in our work habits has a negative impact on those around us? Unfortunately, years of training can be wasted because we will give up on a person and assume that he has no ability to be trained differently. So let me take you through a checklist of items I think are important to reverse the years of negative thinking.

- The first is to realize that "**quality is first**". No matter what we do in our environment, we have to deliver quality. For me, it is simple. When people continue to do business with you, when people continue to let you lead them, when children respect you as a parent and when your partner loves you as a mate, then quality has been delivered.

- The second is **"to know that desire creates power"**.

Power does not come from money, privilege or position, it comes from a desire to achieve to the next level time and time again.

- Third, **"expect to win"**. There are people in business or in life who start off with this comment, "Well, tell me the worse case scenario and then I can deal with the rest." I think that is an inappropriate and irresponsible comment. I do not want to know the worse case scenario. It doesn't matter to me. If it happens, we'll deal with it. We must expect to win. You cannot go into any life situation expecting to lose.

- The fourth is **"the realization that action conquers fear"**. When we are immobilized by fear, we are incapable of positive action. There are a lot of people who truly fear success. Those individuals can work on a project or a program for long periods of time until it is time for the final decision, then they find a reason to destroy the work they have accomplished. **Action conquers fear, and activity breeds success**. In sales or any profession often people fail due to lack of activity. If people are trying to accomplish goals and if they have a clear mission from the leadership, activity will, in turn, breed success.

There is a saying, "I have known salespeople who were liars, gamblers and cheats, but I have never known a successful salesperson who has sat on his butt all day."

- Fifth, **"in the middle of every difficulty lies an opportunity"**. This is not only easy to say but easy to accomplish. It separates positive from negative. It separates over-achievement from the average.

- Sixth, **"success is a journey not a destination"**. When I was a bill collector, I had little or no focus. The focus was simply locate the individual, collect the money and return to base. Later, when I started to build clients in the non-profit and for-profit sectors, I started to define success differently. I got caught up in their drive and determination to serve others. That is why I often think service organizations miss the obvious, which is, we must help our clients meet the needs of their clients. We have to look at the skill packages that we bring to the table and how our clients can utilize them and our relationships to better serve their clients.

Hopefully, this book on creating reality will give you the ability and appreciation of weaving all of our experiences by a common thread. Creating reality not only drives the individual, but it drives everyone around us.

- Seventh, **"never, never quit at anything, anytime, anywhere"**. In 1984, I proposed that our organization become involved in risk management services. This was highly unusual for our company and was a big leap from the types of services we previously offered our clients. I will never forget that day because after I gave my idea, an individual who is no longer with our organization began to laugh. But one man, the owner of the organization, thought about it and believed with me that it was possible. It took years of persistence and discipline to turn this idea into reality. Today, Risk Management is a profitable division of our organization that delivers a nationwide service to our clients.

I was fortunate to work with an individual who is not only the owner of the organization, but a dear friend. I had the advantage over others by being around a mentor who had the vision and creativity to take risks on new concepts and ideas.

Even if all the pieces are in place to create and motivate, a leader still needs one critical element and that is someone who believes in him. For the last seventeen years, I have been blessed to have as my friend and colleague, William Lehr. Never once did Bill fail to believe that what we were attempting was possible. He was always there to listen, counsel and advise. There are always situations when you cannot stand alone, and Bill makes sure that does not happen to me. Every leader can fly higher if there is a safety net under him. Bill Lehr made sure the ropes were secure. I have a story that will give you the perfect insight into Bill Lehr. During an office Christmas party, the employees gave Bill a leash and collar to use in an attempt to "control" me. Bill responded, " I would much rather trade this leash and collar for a pair of spurs." Often we manage the way we are managed.

If we are given autonomy and the permission to create, then we must offer those we manage the same privileges.

I am lucky I was blessed with a mentor who had those qualifications. So what we learn emotionally, as well as physically, is to never, never quit.

- The eighth point is "**expect excellence**". **We can't expect excellence in others until we expect excellence in ourselves.** That, however, is not reality based. We are talking in this book about creating reality. Even if we fail, we can expect excellence in others because when they succeed, they will help bring us back from a slump or a slip in attitude that we may have suffered.

- Ninth is that "**our aspirations are our possibilities**". Possibilities do not come from time. What we aspire to – what we hope our children will aspire to – is to help lead the leader. It is always wonderful to speak to a child and ask what he wants to be when he grows up. He will rattle off profession after profession from secret agent to rodeo rider. Have you ever asked yourself why they do that? They do that because they believe that all those aspirations are possible. I love to tell my children when they visualize multiple careers, they can be all of those professionals. As adults, we must never grow up past our dreams. I believe Dad and the Alexander Cortezzos of the world never grew up. They had this inner child-like quality that overpowered the adult that was trying to mature and grow up. Once for Father's Day just a few years before my dad passed away, I bought him a new baseball glove. I put a card with it that said, "Dad, I hope that you never lose that child within you that can throw and catch a ball." I have pictures of him playing catch with Anthony, Jr., who was either eight or nine at the time. As sick as my dad was and as sore as his arm was, he was still able to throw and catch with my son because his aspiration to play with a grandson created the possibility of playing through pain.

- Tenth is, **"I believe we are what we think about"** and if we think about success, motivation, attitude and optimism, they are what we will become and obtain.

- And finally, **"no goals, no glory"**. I believe goals are glory and I believe glory has many faces. The under-thinkers create a reality that is not glorious but merely functional; but the over-thinkers, dreamers and risk takers are the ones that stand and deliver. They know they are the dream, the smell of success, the talk of accomplishment and the walk of champions. They are the people who create reality and build the dreams.

XVII

PEOPLE WE ALL KNOW

XVII

PEOPLE WE ALL KNOW

T here are several special productivity problems that are caused by people or events. Let's visit the types of people that can hurt productivity, create negative morale and pessimism within an organization. Remember, the responsibility of a leader is to monitor all types of personalities no matter how tough the case may appear.

- First is the negative employee. This is the employee who sees everything through a pessimistic view. No matter how good the situation may be, he or she always finds a negative aspect to focus on. Negative employees are the type of people that appear to be happy only when they are miserable. Negative employees can also be a counterbalance because you can rely on them to tell you the worse case scenario, therefore, you don't have to spend as much time researching the downside because they will gladly let you know what it is.

- Second are the hostile employees. They come from many sources, but usually from a lack of recognition for their performances. They can become bitter and resentful. Leaders should spend time with hostile employees and try to nurture a relationship because they can be turned around and become very productive.

- Third are deadline missers. These are individuals who always volunteer for projects, but rarely make the deadline in the appropriate time frame. They always have reasons why they were not able to accomplish what they were suppose to do and often it can be tracked to a fear of success. They are okay as long as their work can be performed in a risk-free environment. When the time comes for risk taking, they may miss a deadline on purpose because of the fear of success or failure.

- Fourth is the careless employee. This employee or colleague can cause a great deal of havoc in an organization. Careless employees lack a sense of purpose, sense of urgency and mission. If they can be mentored into having a personal mission and vision statement, they, like the hostile employee, can be turned around. Once motivated, they develop strong skill packages.

- Fifth, are lazy employees. They are the most difficult to motivate and the most challenging to mentor. You may be dealing with years of inability to achieve and you have to scrape through those layers of inactivity to find their true skill packages. However, lazy employees should not be discarded.

Giving them projects or responsibilities in small doses brings them along at an easier pace. This results in these employees finding merit in their work and they are then are able to achieve goals in the future. Chances are this type employee is never going to be highly motivated, but, in certain roles, could be productive for a particular job.

- Sixth, stubborn employees can be fun to work with. They allow you to test your leadership skills by trying to motivate them into the team and into the work process. As exasperating as a stubborn employee can become, he will help us grow as professionals and as managers. The stubborn employee often works best in a team environment or a cooperative system where the team relies on his work being completed. Peer pressure can often have a positive impact on the stubborn employee as well as the careless or lazy one.

- Seventh, there is the pushy employee, who is harnessed and controlled, but can develop into a creative renegade. The issue is he or she may be an overachiever lacking the style and grace to manage or work in an environment that is conducive to getting along with others. The pushy employee can be intimidating, therefore, the weaker managers should not be assigned to him or her since they could be overrun which would have a negative impact on the morale of the staff.

- Eighth is the slow employee. The slow employee, if he produces quality work, may be sheltered by the other team members. This is an individual who needs to be mentored to understand the urgency of projects. Often the slow employee will have patience and, therefore, will become a good trainer or be able to work on projects that have longer time frames.

- Ninth, thin-skinned or sensitive employees are truly the most difficult. No matter what type of constructive criticism is leveled at them, they take it personally and can react in a hostile manner. Many times the thin-skinned may also have other areas which need to be developed, as they can also become hostile, stubborn and pushy. These individuals should not be put into high pressure situations until they have developed a skill package necessary to achieve at a progressive rate.

Remember, that in many problem-solving discussions, we spend too much time discussing how the problem happened and not enough time solving the problem.

It is counterproductive to discuss the weaknesses of employees with those who cannot assist the employee. Problems can occur when employees feel you are talking about them behind their back. You will have even more difficulty trying to motivate them in the future.

XVIII

CORPORATE KINDERGARTEN

XVIII

CORPORATE KINDERGARTEN

In my seminars, I use an actual kindergarten report card to illustrate little has changed for us since age five. The goals we were given in kindergarten continue for us as adults. Let's explore a few corporate lessons that started in kindergarten.

- **"I play well with others and I am a good sport."** This is still critical today in all areas of our endeavors. How often should we be benched in our careers?

- **"I am courteous and considerate of others."** How many companies have failed, how many goals have been crushed because people cannot tolerate the imperfections of others?

- **"I accept and respect authority."** Enough said.

- **"Listen to instructions."** How many times do we instruct an entire team or production unit and of the ten people, each will hear the simple direction a different way?

- **"I follow directions."** Many times people will follow directions until it suits them to do otherwise. If we fail to give them focus and leadership, then it is easier for them not to follow the directions.

- **"I make good use of my time."** How many billions of dollars have been spent on time management? A simple process to learn in kindergarten is to stay focused and concentrate on the task.

- **"I respect the rights and properties of others."** Your office is wherever you stand and you have the right to expand the property of your individual genius.

- **"I work without disturbing others."** How often can we walk through our buildings in our professional workplace and see time being wasted on discussions that have nothing to do with production or positive activity? Everyone is entitled to down-time and socialization, but not when it occurs on a frequency that hurts the delivery of goals.

- **"I think for myself and solve my own problems."** One of the key areas I look for as a leader is the individual who has to ask eight people the same question. It signals a lack of self-confidence and is an area that needs more mentoring. We must become a force of one within a team of many. Eventually, final decisions cannot be made by a committee.

- **"I do work carefully and neatly. I obey school rules."** Everyone has rules and most must be obeyed. Sometimes, though, we need to leave the door open for the application of the corporate renegade style which improves the goal system and increases the achievement of others.

- **"I listen while others speak."** As adults, how often do we become impatient and finish the sentences for others and not clearly hear what they have been saying? We cheat ourselves and the speaker.

- **"I enjoy work and play."** We were told to learn it at age five, but how many of us have failed to put equal amounts of effort into both play and work?

- **"I know my whole name, address and phone number."** You may think this does not have a place as an adult, but it does. There are too many of us who know our whole name and base it on what a title is on a business card. My business card shows no title, because title serves no purpose. It's just a process that puts our ego where our creativity belongs.

- **"I claim only my share of attention."** Enough said.

- **"I rest quietly."** Maybe at age five we are talking about nap time, but there is corporate napping. During corporate napping we sleep through opportunities.

We had a shot at it in kindergarten and we are still trying to learn it today. Let us just try to take it one step at a time. Work on a couple of these issues and go on from there.

XIX

A CHECKLIST FOR THE FUTURE

XIX

A CHECKLIST FOR THE FUTURE

Just like we had a checklist and a report card for evaluation in kindergarten, as professionals we need a checklist that should simply say "The Future". During a sales meeting, I asked everyone to write down one or two words that symbolized the future. Each month we took one of these words and concentrated on it. The words written were passion, guts/courage, challenge, life, create, purpose, never idle, death/life, wisdom, honesty, drive, faith and trust, no fear, at peace and knowledge. We, as individuals, need to have a checklist for the future.

We need a road map that helps us reach our goals and allows us to achieve what others may see as unattainable.

I highly suggest that you conduct this process with your colleagues. We then had the words printed on parchment, framed and hung in the offices of every professional in our organization. It helps us build the right structure. It helps us concentrate on what is important to the entire team. We do not build team concepts and structure by hooking cubicles together, having the same technology and same color that identifies our team. Teams are linked and grow by having a dedication to a common purpose.

People need physical and visual cues to accomplish their challenge and to proceed to future endeavors.

XX

EXPECTATIONS AND OBJECTIONS

XX

EXPECTATIONS AND OBJECTIONS

W hen dealing with others' expectations, we are often faced with issues that force us out of our game plan. Many times we can abandon our vision, our motivation and our personal dynamic marketing plan, because when dealing with others' expectations, they may either be too high or too low. Four techniques I believe to be critical in dealing with others' expectations are:

- **Keep a realistic perspective.** We need to evaluate the expectation that is being placed on us and determine if it is truly realistic. Can we, in a given time frame or by utilizing our skill-package, deliver a realistic result of the expectation being placed on us? Expectations do not only come from individuals, but, perhaps, from entire organizations, families and our personal Board of Directors. If we find, for example, that our personal Board of Directors is placing unrealistic expectations on us, then this is a point where we need to have a retreat planning session and talk about the objectives and how to deliver satisfactory results.

- **Rely on your own organization.** Everyone, whether he is self-employed or employed by others, has an organization around him. We need to rely on the strengths of that organization, its staff and management team, to help us meet the expectations of others. Those professionals, who are unwilling to delegate or feel the only time they can be successful is when they work on issues themselves, can fall prey to trying to meet expectations that are unrealistic. I often learn to rely on our organization. One perfect example happened after I lost a large account due to an acquisition. My client was acquired in a merger and my contracts were not renewed. I received the traditional phone call and was instructed to comply with the transition. I received that phone call while I was in a meeting with some of my risk management colleagues. These colleagues are not your traditional sales professionals. Their role is to handle the loss control and risk management issues of our clients. I was verbalizing my disappointment in losing the client and working through the mathematical gyrations of what this meant to the bottom line while wondering how quickly I would have to replace the account I lost with one of equal or larger size. I was speaking to myself, but out loud, saying that I had to find a client of similar size by September. Two of the risk managers looked at me and said, "No, *we* have to replace that client by September!" I immediately realized that their perception was that this was a team effort. What was expected of me was equally expected of them as well. They made it clear it was okay to rely on them and the organization to help meet the goal of finding a new client. I was immediately comforted and felt like I wasn't alone. The feeling of being in isolation was taken away from me by the fact that a team was in place.

- **Trust your instincts.** We as professionals instinctively come to valid conclusions without a great deal of data to support those instincts. When people are expecting us to deliver, we have an immediate instinct as to whether we will be successful or not. Often we agree to take on a task because of our inability to say no, or to be less than honest with people that our skill package is not sufficient to deliver on their expectations. I believe that marketing is a good example. Often we sit across the table from someone early on in the appointment process or the first interview stage, and we know based on our instincts that this is not going to become successful. We know this to be true when we interview people, have domestic debates, listen to our children and we certainly know it in business dealings. Our instincts are telling us what the expectations are going to be, but we believe that we still have to go through all of the process to simply find the answer we've known all along has been based on our initial instincts.

- **Marketing is a learning experience.** Many people are afraid to discuss their failure. They fear that they will be judged incompetent or weak. Yet it is the marketing of our learning experiences which helps us to see clearly our objectives and where the expectations of others can lead us. I believe there could be a tremendous document written based just on expectation versus delivery, using actual scenarios from individuals to document the data. What a tremendous learning experience it would be for all of us if we would share and market expectations of others and how we dealt with it!

No matter what area of life we enter, we are always going to be faced with objections. The basic technical answer to handling objections, written in all of the marketing and sales books that I have ever read states, "Objections are not really no's, but the fact that we have not met the needs of the person offering the objection." If that was true, then why in my experience, when I had people say no to me was I not successful in my mission? With all due respect to all of the marketers in the country, sometimes no means no. But there is a foundation for handling objections that I think will minimize the rejection process for you in the future.

- **First is to not be afraid to immediately react to the objection.** I believe that one of the best things you can do at the end of a meeting is to ask the participants how they honestly felt the meeting went, to immediately take their temperature. If you sense there is a lack of trust on their parts and they do not believe your proposal, before you leave the meeting, address the issues that had become murky and cloudy.

It is important to react to the objection to be sure you clearly understand it and can adequately build a response.

- **Second is to listen to the objection.** Don't take it personally. Don't feel like the process is over just because you had an objection. Objections are healthy and they're critical to the decision-making process. If you conduct a presentation and no one responds to you, this is a bad day. It is going to make the process much more difficult to be successful. Think about your personal lives. Someone could be angry and upset with you, but let him give you the silent treatment and it is much more difficult with which to deal.

- **The third foundation is to concede.** There are some objections on which we need to concede. No matter what we do in our marketing plan or delivery system we still may have to concede an objection to the individual. This is very healthy and, in fact, builds integrity and honesty into the process.

- **Fourth is to question the objection.** Many times people use standard objections. It is an easy way to create a smoke screen to protect them from having to go deeper into the discussion or address a roadblock that hides the true objections. It is simple, for example, to say that your price was too high, or I wanted the red one or you appear too young to handle my account. All of these objections may be merely hiding the true objection. So, it is important to question the objection so the person who established the objection can make as an informed decision as possible. They will respect you for it, and in fact, they will be encouraged by the process.

- **Fifth is to qualify the objection.** People do not put equal weight to all their objections. Some are minimal and others are major. You need to qualify the objection so you are working with the major issues for the individual. Truly, people verbalize objections as they think of them. We must place objections into a pattern or grid and focus on the major objections developing win-win solutions.

- **Finally, capitalize and close on the objection.** We can all learn a great deal from the way we handle objections. It helps us build on our strengths and minimize our weaknesses. Most importantly, we have to capitalize on the objections. We have to learn from them, have to solve the objection to the best of our ability and then close on the issue.

Once you have handled all the objections that someone has proposed, it is important to ask for the decision.

Whether that decision is favorable or unfavorable to you, at least it is closed and you can move on. Files are littered with dead proposals of marketers and professionals who were unsuccessful because they may have handled the objection, but they could never ask for the close. The term closing is not just a technical term used in sales. We as individuals must bring closure to everything we do. If you think back in your life to the experiences you did not successfully close and put behind you, these are the issues that still follow and haunt you today. People make statements like, "If only I had done this"... or "only done that"; they can name for you the time and place that would have changed their lives.

The reality is that if you don't learn how to make closure part of your personal dynamic marketing plan and part of your personal delivery system, then your career and your personal life will always be filled with open-ended issues and the perception of failure as failures.

XXI

THE PONY EXPRESS RIDES AGAIN

XXI

THE PONY EXPRESS RIDES AGAIN

I want to discuss the current trend of virtual corporation. I believe, to a large degree, it is a trend because few people can work in isolation for long periods of time. It has been my pleasure to work with a sales professional, who is probably the finest, pure sales warrior I have ever known. He excels when it comes to self-discipline and self-motivation. After being with us for many years, he decided to go off and start his own business. What brought him back to our organization was not his failure to succeed. To the contrary, he was very successful in a short period of time. What he missed most was the camaraderie and the ability to interact with others, in success and failure. I believe this holds true for most people.

I believe that virtual corporations will eventually evolve into what we know from history to be the Pony Express. For example, we need to be able to go into a new area or location, set up our delivery system and have it function. What is difficult on the worker is traveling for long periods of time in isolation away from family and colleagues. I believe that a future Pony Express will ride again in business.

One individual will go into a metropolitan area and establish a base of operation, igniting a marketing fire for a particular campaign. Then a new individual on a fresh horse will arrive and continue the process. The first professional is allowed to go back to base to refuel, retool and rest. I think this prospective idea has a real possibility of taking hold in a national delivery system.

Will the Pony Express system I am designing ever become reality? I believe it has already started. I believe that on the heels of virtual corporations rides this Pony Express concept that gives both a quick hitting base of operations and the ability not to lose the individual. Many careers have been destroyed because of a lack of discipline on the road or because workers have been left out too long without any recognition, reward or encouragement.

As we began to expand nationally we found it difficult to be out for long periods of time without being re-supplied. We had to realize our offices were no longer physical structures; our offices were wherever we stood. It brought with it a loneliness that many people face in carving new horizons.

We make marketing and motivation much more difficult then they need to be. It's the ability to realize our roles are not defined by our physical and technological limitations. Our roles are defined by our creativity to serve needs and deliver quality service.

XXII

SALESPERSON ANONYMOUS

XXII

SALESPERSON ANONYMOUS

I created a Salesperson Anonymous Meeting, also known as SAM. I modeled it after AA meetings. I stood up in a sales meeting and said, "Hi. My name is Anthony and I am a salesperson." I went on to say how I made mistakes with a client that caused me to lose a particular deal. We all laughed and had fun with it. Another stood and said, "Hi, I'm John and I'm a salesman, and I need help." We went on to talk about key training issues. Running it like an Alcoholics Anonymous meeting broke down a barrier that is often put up because of office walls, suits, business cards, titles and technology. It brings us down to the bare paint which is that we are humans who, when faced with creating reality, don't always get it right.

The Salesperson Anonymous Meeting gave us a forum to realize our addiction to imperfection.

We became a true team that particular morning because we knew we all stood together.

Whether we are salespeople, parents or professionals there is a closeness, a bond, shared by those who accept challenge. We are linked, we are together, we are the future.

XXIII

THE HARD HAT CLUB

XXIII

THE HARD HAT CLUB

A basic sales force in any corporation sets its sights on improving its own performance and, for competitive reasons, the producers measure their levels of success against those around them. In 1989, I was searching for a way to motivate our sales force with a system that would be fun, yet make a clear point. Often, in business, we take ourselves too seriously and fail to have fun and enjoy the lighter moments. I tried to think of something fun and exciting for our sales force, and in doing so, I created the Hard Hat Club. The Hard Hat Club was founded based on a premise that individuals need to be recognized. What I did was purchase $5 bright yellow hard hats from a local hardware store. I instructed the sales force that once each hit a certain level of production he would receive a hard hat.

In football a player who scores touchdowns receives a sticker on his helmet. Sometimes there is a skull and crossbones for defense and little crowns for offense. I devised my own sticker system. Every year I would come up with a different sticker – always something playful, like little stars, flags and coins. One year it was a scratch and sniff planet Earth. For every increment of production the producers reached, they received stickers on their hard hats. The Hard Hat Club became a motivational club. We would sit around the conference table discussing the production report during the early part of the sales meeting, wearing our hard hats. When a new producer was inducted into the Hard Hat Club, he or she would shake hands with the members and then they would bang helmets together. Their names were put on the front of their helmets. Stickers were awarded and placed on the helmet as goals were met. Worn with pride on the back rim of our hard hats are large heart stickers. Every year a producer makes goal, he receives a heart that is symbolic of the hard work and dedication he put into his job to attain his goals. They would also be invited to an annual conference which usually took place in Atlantic City. While on the Executive Bus on our way to Atlantic City, the Hard Hat Club members made up code names for everyone which became extremely entertaining. Code names such as "Hollywood", "Blaster", "Pig Dog", "Bubba", "Tattoo" and "Vulture" were put on the back of the helmets. The code of silence that was cast upon all Hard Hat Club members prohibits me from explaining to you why some of these names were selected.

The Hard Hat Club became synonymous with other issues. It made it clear to the professionals in the sales force and the entire company, the world of sales and marketing is a game meant to be played hard and enjoyed when played well. We must have fun with our careers and the Hard Hat Club represented grown men and women sitting around a beautiful boardroom in a gorgeous office building wearing the ugliest yellow hard hats with the silliest, child-like stickers placed on them. That $5 piece of plastic became a tremendous motivational tool for a very professional sales force that has been together in excess of twelve years. Besides being a form of motivation, the Hard Hat Club was a tremendous equalizer. Regardless of the corporate rank of the individual, all Hard Hat members were treated the same. It gave us a chance for camaraderie, friendship and respect which usually does not occur between most production team members concerned only with their own individual production.

At the end of every year, the hard hats are collected and put into storage so that the hard hat has to be earned every year by the member. Peer pressure comes to bear, also, since you only have six months to enter the club for that particular year. Sales success is judged by the number of stickers and the array of different symbols that are placed on the helmet.

One item worn on our helmets with great pride is a piece of silver duct tape cut into a shape of a scar, worn on only a few helmets of the Hard Hat Club members present during one monumental sales meeting. I had just read Leadership Techniques of Attila the Hun, a book I highly recommend to everyone. The book talks about how, prior to going into battle, the Huns would take their knives and cut the face of the young Huns. In essence it was saying to them, "Don't fear battle because you are already wounded, already cut and bloodied for battle." What I did was take a roll of duct tape and cut a series of scars to be symbolic of the scars of young Huns. During the sales meeting, I went around the room and placed a piece of duct tape on the faces of all the sales producers. Within a matter of moments, they were mentally transformed from wearing suits to wearing fur garments and horned helmets. Believe me, after the sales meeting they practically ran through the walls to get out and conquer new marketing horizons. In fact, some of their colleagues who were not in the sales meeting pointed out to them that they were wearing duct tape on their face. In turn, the producers explained to the office staff that it wasn't duct tape, but a scar given to them by the Hun leader and that they were preparing for battle. Needless to say, there was some concern for the mental stability of the sales force, and in particular, its sales manager. The tape scars were a symbolic and fun way to show that marketing is a game we play and it should be enjoyed.

I think all salespeople, professionals and leaders realize that there is no success without sacrifice.

Most books written fail to note the personal sacrifice it takes to be successful in a business environment. Often that sacrifice entails having to travel and be away from our families. It requires working in isolation, being disciplined outside of our normal office environment and having to face scenarios that demand our attention quickly and at a moments notice.

If the Hard Hat Club has taught me anything, it has taught me how critically important it is to always be creative in a world that is, for the most part, extremely structured. Think about the majority of people you know. How many people can be served a piece of pie without eating the point first? In a restaurant even servers assist us by turning the point of the pie toward us. We are a society that has been conditioned to line up for everything. We follow a very uniform structure. We always face with our heads up, watching the numbers in the front of elevators. We always face the same way in lines and certainly eating pie is an example of how structured we are in our society.

Creating our own reality and building creativity helps us break the structure and create the vision that helps us reach the pinnacle of greatness.

XXIV

SCORING A GOAL

XXIV

SCORING A GOAL

For leaders, the religion of goal achievement is paramount to our success. To achieve a goal is to create a whisper of fire in your soul.

Goals are the internal energy that will propel a professional to success. Goals create the future of an organization and the well being of a family. We have no right to question the goals of our children if we constantly fall short of our own goals.

Everyone must achieve to their potential; we cannot count on someone else to deliver our future and dream our dreams for us.

We have an opportunity for the future that most people can never realize in their lifetimes. Together, we can strive to reach heights that, before, seemed too high for us. We can set examples for our families and all those who follow in our steps.

The goal process can never be taken lightly; it is not one of those measures that become commonplace. To cheat on your goal is to rob your heritage and desecrate the foundation of the overachievers who came before us.

We are not like everyone who plays our game. We are the creators and visionaries of the goals of others. If we take our goals lightly, we short-arm the future for those we lead.

Every moment we fail to support each other and second-guess our achievement, we prevent the survival and success of the system. No matter where we go, goals follow us and bang loudly on our souls.

In the end, it was never the goals that drove us, it was always the need, desire and courage to conquer them. To take them lightly is to assume we were never here at all.

You can monitor a leader's pulse rate by goals per minute.

I know people who do not understand what a goal is. Some people confuse goals with action plans. A goal is a dream, but it has an ending point. You are going to get there, but how long will it take you? I have to break it to you, we may only have six minutes to get a goal accomplished as there may be no long-term opportunity. Short-term is nothing more than putting some kind of a quantifier on the goal, thus it has to be done in a realistically fast period of time. Long-term is a vision of the future built on a foundation of successful short-term goals.

Discussing our goals with others is one of the most successful ways of dealing with achievement and staying focused. Tell people what you are trying to accomplish. It puts a subtle pressure on us when we tell someone we now have to deliver; it helps people point us in the right direction. It is critically important we follow through using direct action to take steps to continue forward; we do not want to process items over and over again. Planning is the glue to our goal process; it binds our mission and focus. Planning is a thoughtful process that brings our goals to conclusions.

When we form our goal structure, we have to keep in mind that, although we have to be successful at what we create, we also want to challenge ourselves to be better than we are currently. So it is important that we set short and long-term goals that are a challenge to us. Goals must force us to stretch and to achieve in areas where we have not been successful or we have not attempted to penetrate in the past. If we are honest with ourselves, a good way to define our dreams is that "dreams are goals with deadlines". We have to put in the ability to plan, to look at short-term and long-term goals and have the ability to change. I have found what stops most people from achieving success is their inability to change and try new endeavors.

Change is for everyone but evolution is for the motivated.

So much has been written about goal setting and how critical it is for organizations and individuals to set goals, yet rarely are we very clear on how to implement the goal process. As I discussed before, visualization is critical in goal planning.

We must project ourselves into the future in order to set our goals today.

One of the most useful ways to set goals is to understand the entire planning process. People immediately think in terms of one to five years, but what really forces creativity into a structured world is to plan several years into the future. Personally, I like to plan fifteen years ahead where I believe I will be as an individual and where an organization will be as a corporate entity. Not restricting myself to five years greatly expands the visualization process.

People respond to planning. They feel comfortable and safe if someone has a vision for the future. Although the vision will certainly change and develop as the years progress, it gives direction and it makes the process easier by building the goals and systems around a vision and a plan.

The process is easier than you think. If you build on your strengths, both personally and professionally, you are then able to project how things will look in the future based on those same strengths. It is not necessary to abandon your current delivery system, but, merely, be able to expand upon it. Based on your current planning and goal-setting methods, you can project what the environment will look like in the future.

You will be pleasantly surprised how people will attach themselves to your vision and dream. If people are not going to believe in the dream and vision now, they certainly are not going to follow the goal-setting process in the future. If they have a chance to debate and discuss the vision in multiple year intervals, then, as the system begins to evolve, they have more of a comfort level with the entire process. People will be willing to take risks and support your entrepreneurial spirit because they were involved in the goal planning process. If they see leaders planning well into the future, they feel compelled as individuals to plan for their own future. Their goals become more aggressive and challenging to them as professionals. What you create as you build your structure into the future are groups of people on the same developmental wave length. Everyone works toward a common goal. In time, the goal setting process is no longer six months or three years; it can become generations long. People will then surround themselves with colleagues who can replace their current duties so that they are free to obtain future success.

I have found few individuals can really plan for the future and build their own perpetuation plans. Many talk of it, but few can truly deliver a solid functional plan. It is always difficult to give up something you have mastered. But we know, as professionals, unless we do that we cannot follow our plan and vision for the future. Part of the planning process and part of the goal-setting environment is to decide early on who those individuals will be that you will need to surround yourself with to accomplish your tasks. At our organization, we have colleagues who are driven and dedicated. Even though they may lack the overall picture of the entire company, they focus on their particular area of expertise. These people are the pieces of the professional puzzle. Without them, the delivery system would fail, but with them change and creativity is common and cherished. Many people are surprised when they fail at goals or fail to achieve their level of goal-setting processes because there is some external or internal reasons that caused the process to break down. In reality, they did not install the proper team to help them achieve their goals. They relied solely on their ability and instinct which may be sufficient in a short-term goal process, but inappropriate for the long-term. Certainly as we get older, we realize that we need to have creative talent around us in order to support our long-range planning process. If not, it's no different than being on a construction site and having the most high-powered equipment tunnel trench after trench. The tunneling process goes very quickly, but when you stop the machinery and turn around, you notice that no one has been laying pipe and backfilling the ditch. Therefore, we realize planning and goal setting go hand in hand. **We are planning not only as individuals but as entire corporations.**

We are force of one in a team of many.

XXV

THE LEAD IN LEADERSHIP

XXV

THE LEAD IN LEADERSHIP

There are certain aspects of leadership that propel us to be effective in our roles as managers and leaders. No matter what our position, we struggle with self-awareness, managing stress and creative problem-solving. As leaders, we can tend to force ourselves on people. My personal mission statement is to be a welcomed leader in any arena I choose to stand. I believe the key word is <u>welcomed</u>. If we are too hard-driving or tenacious, we will offend people and make it difficult for them to respond to our vision. As leaders, we must strive for dependability. Show people they can depend on our consistent professional behavior. We have a stewardship responsibility to morally do the proper thing and watch over what is under our control.

The worse thing you can do as a leader is to fail to praise people when they have done a good job. Whether they write a letter, design a brochure, work on a program or coordinate a reception, people want recognition more than they want money. People want to feel good about themselves. They want to know that all their hard work and effort made a difference. As I said before, be very kind to the people you see on the way up because they are the same people you see on the way down. They are waiting for you to come right back down the ladder and are praying that you go down past them again. So, always congratulate someone for doing a good job.

Many managers and leaders have the problem of being indecisive. They can't make a decision and stick with it. They are swayed by the last person to stand in front of them, since they have a distaste for communicating difficult decisions. Don't be afraid to say what everyone is thinking. People appreciate leaders with the courage to address tough issues.

Inform others of your decisions and tell them what you are going to do. Some leaders make decisions, but they don't communicate them. They then wonder why people don't follow them. Some leaders are decisive to themselves, but they are afraid to communicate it because they are concerned that people will be confrontational. When you make a decision, tell people and follow through with direct action.

The best thing you can say to somebody is that you need him. Find personal motivation in each person you lead and then talk with that person sincerely about his or her issue. Great managers take time to know their people. Leadership is action, not position. Employees need to know you can do it and they need to know you are challenging yourself as you seek to challenge them. You have to go out now and challenge yourself so they will follow and respect you. Get them to follow you now to a different horizon. That's why I say action, not position, is the framework for leadership.

It was taught to me that a leader takes more than his share of the blame and less than his share of the credit. When a problem occurs, look to take the blame as their leader. Immediately give them the credit when the situation is successful. Then never forget the biggest and most important asset of any corporation is the respect that its leaders are given by their clients, business partners and employees.

XXVI

HANDLING MONKEYS

XXVI

HANDLING MONKEYS

I learned from several business leaders to refer to problems as monkeys on our back.

There are seven rules I follow when handling monkeys. They fit all monkeys regardless of species.

First, **"Monkeys should be fed or shot"**, meaning when problems occur we must work the problem, remove it, or deal with it immediately. The tendency is to put it aside because it may be a tough problem. I suggest the minute you get a problem, either feed it or shoot it. Feeding is to analyze the problem which may require you to get more background on how to best handle it or dump it. What I mean by shooting it is to delegate it, give the problem to someone better equipped to handle it or develop additional research.

"A maximum number of monkeys shall be set" means that we can only handle so many problems and then the load gets beyond us. You have to know as a professional how many problems you can deal with. Now reality is that often we can't control the flow of monkeys. You can have a real bad day and get hit with several problems at one time, or you may go for a month and have only a few. Either way, you have to know what your threshold is. Once you identify your threshold of problem solving, you will want to use your core group and the people around you to help you deal with the problems.

Third, **"Staff shall be responsible for taking the initiative when it comes to feeding"**. You don't want people who get a problem, and the first thing they do is stand with a monkey outside your door. Or, besides coming to see you with it, they are going to bother all their other colleagues with the same problem, looking for assistance, or someone else to sample the "whine". You want your staff to be responsible for taking initiative, or at least coming to you with a solution. You should be saying to your people, "What have you done to feed it or kill it and do you have any solutions?" The best thing out of your mouth at that point should be, "How do you feel about this or what would you do about this?" Sometimes their answers are better than yours.

"Monkey feeding appointments may be rescheduled, but never postponed indefinitely." If you have a problem, deal with it. Someone says to you, "We have a problem and people are coming here at two o'clock, they are hot, hostile, want an answer, and they are really upset." Now, you may not be prepared for two o'clock. In fact, it could be a reverse problem delete if you see them at two o'clock unprepared, you could have a worse situation. So, you may want to postpone it, but don't postpone it for a week or a month. Solve the problem quickly. The more time wasted, the more inflamed the environment becomes. The colder the trail, the harder to track the monkey.

There is a real tendency among monkey-keepers to discuss monkeys with people who are not part of the solution. When you gossip about monkeys they get mean. It happens all the time. People come in and say, "You are not going to believe what Bob did." So, I say, "Let's go get Bob." "Well, I have to tell you first." "But we will be hearing only your side of it." There are people – corporate gossip mongers – who enjoy getting dirt on other people. They want to hear and pass all the inflammatory issues. Then you go talk to Bob, listen to his side, and you discover it wasn't even a monkey. It was a personal thing between the two monkey keepers. Monkey keepers are not necessarily good monkey trainers.

"Monkeys shall either be fed face to face or via the phone, not by mail." It is always best to eyeball somebody. Let me tell you why. It's better because people always want conflict to end. People don't like conflict to continue; they don't like to be in a hostile environment. People want issues to be over with. The worst thing that can happen to you is the monkey getting out of control to the point where all sorts of problems are brought up that don't even relate to the true issue. I know that if I have a problem and somebody responds in writing to me – I expect a phone call. At least have the courage to say, "Here's what's going on and how do you feel about it?" Often they will drop mail on you and they think the problem will go away. All that does is make the situation worse. In business, you will lose customers that way. You will lose clients and employees through impersonal correspondence. I dislike monkey keepers who address the monkey from mail, e-mail, memos, or voicemail. They would be of better service if they got in the cage with the monkey. After all, most monkeys only copy our behavior.

"Monkeys or reports on monkeys shall be condensed to one page or less." If people can't give you a problem and lay it out in a page or less, they have not thought it through. They are rambling and not looking for solutions. They are just trying to give it to you and you are not going to be an effective leader if you solve problems for everybody. The tendency with young leaders and managers is their desire to show a reputation and an image that they are problem-solvers. Someone states "Oh, I can handle it" because he wants to establish credibility. All you are doing is undermining the basic instinct that people have to help themselves. This will not occur if you constantly train their monkey.

Every monkey should purchase a "Casualty Insurance Policy" because some monkeys, regardless of training, will become casualties. The reason I write it this way is so you know how to escape from problems. One of my colleagues is a senior member and has been with the company over ten years. He has an account that happens to be a hospital. The hospital has become totally unreasonable. He has jumped through hoops for these people. He has responded to a large amount of changes and requests. He said, "I've got a monkey, the people are unreasonable and I am at the end of my rope." I responded, "What do you want to do?" My colleague replied, "If it's not going well tomorrow, I'll explain to them that we are at the end of our rope and we have done our best. If they don't like it, it's over and they can find somebody else." He knew what his monkey was, he had a solution and he came to me for approval of his solution or suggest another alternative. The worse thing I could say is, "Please, don't do that. It's ridiculous." It's emotional for him, he's in a fire fight. So, when your people come to you, support them, unless their answer is inappropriate or irresponsible. You can't just send them off on their own; that's just ignoring the monkey. If the deal needs to be saved, you need to go along. That's the difference between a boss and a leader. The boss would say, "Don't do that. It's inappropriate." A leader would say, "I'll go with you." We decided he was correct in his decision. The revenue was not worth having one of your best people upset or frustrated because the truth is, if he does not walk away from this monkey, he's not going to take care of it properly. He's not going to feed it because he wants to shoot it, and he's going to set that monkey up to fall. Better he gets out of the deal. When you get into that type of environment, you almost always want to kill it and walk away from the deal because, once you start getting that sour feeling, you'll never treat the client or your co-worker the same. In my experience, when a monkey really goes south on you, you ship the monkey to another zoo.

XXVII

LEADING A SUCCESSFUL TEAM

XXVII

LEADING A SUCCESSFUL TEAM

The concept of team building is one of the hottest topics. But let's get to the heart of teams. Behind every great team, is a great team leader. Teams that have weak leadership fail. Period! The team concept works because it allows efficient and high-speed sub-companies to function inside the large corporate umbrella. Each team develops its own style, training methods, client base and a cohesive effort among the team members. What often is not discussed is the fact that, in the team, you are going to have overachievers and underachievers. The overachievers have to have the ability to motivate and inspire and, if necessary, retire the underachiever in the team. You hone the team to the point that it is an efficient machine concentrating on productive efforts. If you fail to remove the underachievers, you will continue to throw warm bodies at the problem, overextend the team and create corporate bureaucracy.

Team training is critical. Each team member has to be cross-trained in the responsibilities and duties of others in order to support the team when they face crises.

Lack of training has a major impact on confidence. Often organizations fail to train employees properly. The days of on-the-job training are over due to the competition to serve clients. Both management and staff must monitor team goals and the quality of work. Employee turnovers cost both client satisfaction and organizational profits.

We have to remember that people, whether in a team concept or another model, are still faced with a high level of stress that continues to build on them as professionals, family members, parents and friends. I was involved in the evaluation of a company that had a heavy female employee base. What I discovered was that many of them were the heads of their households and also operating as professionals in the business world. We have to be sensitive to their needs in order to help people meet the demands of their jobs plus the demands of their homes. If not, we place people in the situation of having to be in a race that has an ever receding finish line. We make it tougher and tougher for them to attain their goals and still maintain their mental health.

XXVIII

BUILDING AN ORIENTATION TEAM

XXVIII

BUILDING AN ORIENTATION TEAM

An extremely important concept is the orientation team. Without creating an orientation team, you, as a leader, will have difficulty handling all your responsibilities.

> **Today's leader can't be inundated with an over-abundance of baggage or responsibility that cannot be delegated.**

You want to build an orientation team around yourself. This is different from a personal Board of Directors, or traditional management teams. This is a team that understands the corporate goals and can maneuver in negotiations, proposals, new ventures and opportunities. In its purest form, the orientation team can visit a third party and profile your organization into an understandable and attractive package. They will have a common focus, common culture, mission and delivery.

The best way to mentor colleagues is to instill a feeling of confidence in the group that they have a primary focus to their own area of expertise. Later, you can train them to take on more and more responsibilities. Suppose we have an orientation team of four people, representing finance, marketing, operations and customer service. Each speaks about his own area of expertise to a potential client. In large meetings they gain confidence and support from the team. Eventually, the team may split to handle more volume, with team members handling more than one function. In the future, team members will duplicate themselves and the organization creates a system that will improve throughout time.

No matter how long people work together, they rarely have the same mission or the same purpose. However, an orientation team will learn to think as one unit, will learn to move in unison and will anticipate each other's thoughts. You want to create a concurrent mission and purpose. There are covert activities which the orientation team will need to conduct. These covert activities include that they act like an intelligence unit; they move on a mission. **As a leader, the ability to gather intelligence is essential and real**.

What an orientation team can do for you is build momentum. I thought back to my mother, the leader of my first orientation team.

By far, the truest form of momentum is a mother's momentum.

When I was a boy, I always thought of my mom as being a very hard worker. As I got older, I started to put three things together – what I knew as a boy, what I learned about people and what I know about my own professional position. My mother worked long hours sewing blouses in a garment mill. I can remember the noise in that place, the humming, the droning and I can still see my mom with her head down pushing blouses through the machine. That job, today, would be considered so tedious and monotonous, that most would never entertain that kind of work environment. Every day, for twenty years, she had to sustain her momentum. Think about it, for twenty years she worked like that; every day, momentum was necessary to continue her monotonous job. A person in that work environment has to have incredible momentum just to overcome the boredom and the tediousness of the job. People like my mom have creative imaginations. They had to remove themselves mentally from the drone of the job. I could remember my mom being a woman who always had options. Whenever there was a crisis, no matter what the situation, it was my mother, the seamstress, who had options. I remember her having more options than some professional people because her life was built on sustaining and creating momentum. She had to have options to take herself out of the tediousness of the job. Here is a woman who lost her mother at age twelve, and was told by her father to quit high school and stay home to raise her younger brother and sister. Therefore, forget business, forget what your mentors are going to tell you, think like Mom and the momentum of the blue collar worker. They teach lessons of sustained momentum and energy systems that must operate daily. We have a great deal to learn from them. Often they can be more creative than any business executive.

I believe in a Public Creations Department versus a Public Relations Department. Your orientation team must be able to create a vision and then explain it to others. A public relations department does nothing more than take what has occurred and package it for delivery. They take product or service and send it through the delivery system. But a public creations department has to build something from scratch. The leader may envision the process, but it is hard for one person to create, package and deliver. The harder it is to be creative, the more people you need to have around you who are sensitive to your passion and understand your vision. In business, if people do not know the goals and vision, it will be difficult for them to be creative. Everyone has a talent that can support the mission. Followers can then become leaders. In an orientation team, you build leaders to replace you, allowing yourself the freedom to face new challenges.

A sense of teamwork is critical whether you are a leader or a team member. You must instill a sense of teamwork into all the people of the delivery system. Don't get trapped into thinking the team concept is a new one. The team concept has always been around and special senses apply:

- **Sense of teamwork.** Even the most creative, energetic leader needs others to be successful.

- **Sense of client service.** No matter what delivery system you select as a leader, the client has the final decision. An example of this is happening in managed care. Everyone in the system, doctors, hospitals and providers are trying to figure out what the best managed care system is. Guess who will decide – the client. The client, in any delivery system, decides what he will tolerate and what he won't. He will dictate the final system. Always have a sense of client service. Whatever your profession, you have to think like a marketer. The marketer is the one you must protect. Usually he is the most sensitive member on your team. He is adaptable, sociable and blends to multiple arenas. He is not superficial and genuinely cares about people. He is also susceptible to isolation and personal rejection. As a leader, you must protect your marketer and you must nurture your sales force.

- **Sense of specialization.** No matter how broad-based your company, there is a specialization or niche you must create to be successful. In a business portfolio of twenty items, be sure you have a drop-dead perfect delivery on your core products. Be the go-to person in your organization for those areas. Learn them well. Be the expert in a particular area. You will have security and confidence. "The future ain't what it used to be," Casey Stengle said.

Our future is formed by our present creations.

- **Every corporation needs a sense of humor.** I found a way to inject humor fourteen years ago at the office Christmas party. We had a very conservative party consisting of a luncheon and gift exchange. I found the event a bit serious for my taste. Therefore, I started the exchanging of gifts by "Santa". I would play Santa and hand out the employee gifts. The next year I was an Elf which included everything from the rubber shoes with the curled up toes to the pointed little ears. The "elf" would tell humorous stories about each employee. It was like a corporate roast. The third year I dressed up like Mrs. Claus in a Santa suit, a little gray wig, granny glasses and a hat. Another year, I was a corporate angel wearing a white suit with big wings and trumpet. For my final act, I was a mind reader. In each of those instances I could be humorous because the situation allowed it. I could remove the Christmas costumes and become management again. Wherever you work, humor is an integral part of business. You have to have fun as long as you don't do it at the expense of other people.

Humor is important if people start taking themselves too seriously. A good leader can sense when his people need to be motivated and even a bit pampered. For example, if your company is faced with a major change it may be a good time to have an entertaining diversion. Our social committee during a construction project, organized a corporate trivia contest. It created team building and diverted stress. People focused on the game and not the inconvenience due to renovations.

- **Effective leadership behavior.** It is the psychology of the leader that has a positive or a negative impact on the psychology of the people he leads. Often leadership training concentrates on understanding the psychology of others and managing according to others' psychological make-ups. That is impossible – it is better to find the common enemy. You want the employees or the colleagues to focus on one enemy at a time, whether it is a competitor, or a certain type of environment. Always find a common enemy they can focus on and form a structure of teamwork.

We must constantly reinforce the vision. You can't do this enough. I have trouble with constantly reinforcing the vision to my colleagues. I show it to them and talk about it in employee meetings and have all the right communication techniques, but then you get busy and you forget to monitor your vision. They just didn't get it after only learning it three times. You have to constantly reinforce the vision and mission. People struggle, and sometimes you will be seen as arrogant, but don't get spooked by that. Some people fight vision and change, and they are only happy when they are complaining. Generate commitment throughout the group and assist them to concentrate and demonstrate that they are backing the dream. Turn students into teachers, and as leaders, you should turn those you teach into teachers themselves. This is tricky but necessary to be an effective mediator.

The essence of a leader is a mediator with both the mind of a manager and the heart of a negotiator.

If you are a negotiator, find win-win solutions. Remember, both negotiation and mediation, when blended in the discussion, provide equal opportunity for a win-win solution. But a mediator forces compromise. You get the best case scenario. It may not be exactly what both parties wanted, but it works through mediation. You've provided for both the individual and the team. It is hard to be concerned about each man and woman you deal with when locked in negotiations. You can struggle between the happiness of the individual and the team. The issues become:

- Are the results there?
- Are we productive?
- Are both the team and the team members rewarded and recognized?

We never want to leave quality people behind because we cared only about the team and not enough for the individual.

XXIX

ARE THEY BETTER FOR HAVING MET YOU?

XXIX

ARE THEY BETTER FOR HAVING MET YOU?

I always feel like I hit the lottery when I travel on business and I upgrade to first class. One of my favorite amenities about flying first class is when the flight attendant appears with a tray of hot, steaming white rags otherwise known as the "hot towels". Grown men and women wait impatiently for the tray to appear so they can clutch their hot towel and wipe their face and hands. If I was to walk through our building with a tray of hot towels, I imagine my colleagues would look at me very strangely. Yet, in a first class cabin of an aircraft, it is one of the major joys of life. We have to seek out the hot towel for our colleagues and clients. Creativity is necessary to make our clients feel special. We have to look for the hot towel in our environment. As professionals, we are the flight attendants for our first class clients. What hot towel will you serve so they are better for having met you?

Often, we go into a situation with selfish needs in mind. We have our own agenda, whether open or hidden, that accentuates what we want to occur. True professionalism is derived from the belief that if people are better for having met us, satisfaction will come to all parties. I think it's important that we go into every engagement thinking along the lines of people being better because of us. We must convey to people that, whether we do business or not, they can feel free to call us for advice or question us on areas they know to be our strengths. Often, the door is only temporarily closed and it can be opened later by people having honest discussions. Far too many marketers and professionals lose track of potential clients because, once the door is closed, they never attempt to reopen it. If you leave people better for having met you, they feel comfortable with calling and asking for your advice. I try to treat everyone as I would a good friend. Being involved in giving advice and consultation won't break you financially, but can create long-term fans. I believe it is a foundation for integrity and a basis for all relationships.

We must realize how short of a time we have to make a difference. This was illustrated one particular morning for our salespeople.

It was our monthly sales meeting for all production personnel. When I entered the room, I could sense the energy and excitement. The room was alive with animated conversation. Our sales force had successfully reached its goals for the past ten years and this year was going to be equally successful. We were 10-0 and the room was filled with refined arrogance.

I opened the meeting by praising each professional. I asked them to stand while I spoke of their recent success. They were all pumped up and proud of their achievement. I began to explain the pressure of being 10-0 and the desire of competitors to defeat us. As I announced each team member, the group cheered and applauded. Everyone was on their feet and the boardroom was transformed into a locker room.

I picked up a box from the floor and began to fill it with their meeting materials. I placed a hard hat, sales reports and manuals inside the box. On the outside I had written in large letters simply "The Box". We were all on our feet and I asked them to follow me outside the building. I scooped up the box and led them outside. I placed the box on the ground and with a swift motion, kicked the box and sent it flying into the parking lot. Everyone froze and stared at me, totally confused by the turn of events. I spoke in a loud voice and told them they were through and to get out.

Voluntarily or involuntarily eventually everyone gets "The Box". I wanted to dramatize for them that we all someday pack our "Box" and leave our organization.

We returned to the boardroom and discussed our guardianship of "The Box", and what little time we have to make a difference. Regardless if you are 10-0 and undefeated, you must make a difference every day. Our "Box" must be filled with drive, determination and discipline to achieve the pinnacle of greatness.

The sales force has been more driven than ever since that day, because now they realize a sense of urgency for ourselves and our mission. On that particular morning with our material laying in the parking lot we all understood the meaning of thinking outside "The Box". The message is clear, think outside "The Box" or leave with one filled with broken dreams. If we place creativity and energy in our "Box", then we never lay it down; we merely pass it to the next dreamer.

We must think outside our box or someday leave with a box empty of achievement.

XXX

ROB ROUTINE TO REACH REALITY

XXX

ROB ROUTINE TO REACH REALITY

There is a zone that permits only the focus of the future – you have reached it when routine is quick and disposable.

L eaders who consistently deliver a professional performance are in a ZONE. They are in this space that very few people reach. Emotionally, spiritually, they are in a ZONE. Routine to a leader is quick and easily disposed of by delegation and functionality. Leaders focus on creativity which breeds new routine. They move through routine to reach reality. They dispose of the ordinary to accomplish the extraordinary. They bore of the route called routine. Leaders delegate routine in order to create the future. That's when you know you have entered your ZONE. If you are still focusing on the routine, if routine occupies your time and your thought process, then you are not in your ZONE. The routine becomes your job and you lose all directions to the ZONE.

Most people just conform. They do what is expected and attach themselves to others' missions and goals. They are delivery personnel for another person's message. Brainstorming is when a person thinks beyond the conformity. You take the normal course plotted by others and apply different thoughts and creativity. The fun is actually watching yourself spin tasks into success.

Everybody will eventually work in a team environment. People worry about violating team guidelines, whether they are corporate guidelines or just inherent in the team itself. Interpersonal relationships can suffer if you violate team guidelines because individuals need to adhere to a blueprint of the basics. In every arena you enter, there are cliques. You cannot stop cliques from developing. Your job is to utilize them to be productive for you because they have deliverable power behind them. There is going to be competition among team members and disagreements between leaders. But as a leader you must harness corporate cliques to increase their collective energy producing positive versus negative results.

No matter what your role, you are going to have to work and play well with other children. You can't rely on the team clique to deliver your happiness in a workplace. People sometimes get confused. You still have the power of the individual who is responsible for taking care of himself or herself. The team is the delivery system. The team can help you, but it can't be responsible for your own personal success. You still have to be a driver and overachiever. There are people who are over achievers, but when they get into a group setting they somehow fizzle because they are waiting for everyone to perform the same way. When it doesn't happen, they jeopardize their own careers because they do not want to move without the team. They become too much of team players. You have to show intense leadership in a team setting to make sure the work gets accomplished and the goals and mission are satisfied. Fight to ensure the individual's identity is not lost in the shuffle of the creative cards.

Power and influence have a major impact on professionals. There are two kinds: personal power and position power. The better you are at your job, the more effective you are as a leader, the less you rely on position for power. In the beginning, however, position plays an important part. As you move up the corporate ladder, position will have an impact on you and others around you. People treat you differently because of a title or promotion, even though you are the same person. They treat you differently because, often, it is proven that in our new position we act differently. However, once we are in leadership roles, modifications are needed so we can create personal power which comes from expertise. You have to be the best at what you do in order to maintain personal power.

There is a personal attraction, and I am not talking about looks. People are attracted to you because of the way you operate and the kind of leader you are. There are those who will talk behind your back and perhaps fear you. But better they focus negative comments on you than their fellow workers. Charles Curie once gave me a print of General Longstreet at Gettysburg titled the "Loneliness of Command".

You cannot always be loved or liked, but as leaders we must strive to always be followed.

It is the unpredictable, demanding and challenging people who receive the largest following. Everyone has the desire to be a forceful, decisive and fair leader. A leader who is a bit of a tough nut draws people to his mission. In a fight, they can count on you because they know you will not back down. Your effort has to be more focused and more directed than your best efforts the day before. If not, routine and comfort will locate and dominate you.

Position power often gives organizations a false hope that the position alone will create enough of a power base. Position is the ticket to the game, but personality and professionalism gets you a seat up front.

Position merely heats the pot where leadership is cooked and processed.

XXXI

THE INNER KILL

XXXI

THE INNER KILL

The inner kill is a concept relating to the internal and external motivation driving the human being. It can be present in both the overworked and the underworked.

In the overworked, the inner kill occurs when people feel their goals and tasks are unmanageable. They begin to refuse new challenges and let an inner kill begin to destroy their motivation. We all know people who were hard-charging individuals who, after a series of tough challenges, gave up on themselves. They became victims of the inner kill.

The underworked can also fall prey to inner kill. They die from within due to a lack of challenge. Our motivational system cannot function without the fuel of achievement. If we don't challenge ourselves and keep pushing for new achievements, the human being ceases to be stimulated. We are pronounced D.O.A. (Drained of Achievement).

We can prevent the inner kill. By using it to our advantage the inner kill can actually make us stronger. As we conquer our fear of failure or manage difficult tasks, we build up a callous that protects our motivational system. The inner kill will have more layers of confidence to penetrate.

However, it is healthy to maintain the threat of inner kill, because I believe humility comes from the threat. Through humility, we realize our achievement is the result of many people. And it takes our entire support team to defeat the inner kill.

We must walk with kings and not lose the common touch. We have to be able to conduct ourselves in environments where all people can engage us. We must never forget from where we came. If we forget our past, we endanger our future. If we ignore our beginning, we have an inner kill in development.

Our past must ensure our future or success will never come to the present.

Every time we refuse to increase our motivational system we die a little; then we realize the worse form of death is suffocation in our own comfort zone. We must face ourselves and breathe life into our dreams.

XXXII

THE VELVETEEN EXECUTIVE

XXXII

THE VELVETEEN EXECUTIVE

There was a book written that was very popular called <u>The Velveteen Rabbit</u>. The story goes that the velveteen rabbit, when it was new, was the child's favorite toy. But as it got older and played with more often, its fur became matted, the stuffing poked out, one of its eyes wore off and the velveteen rabbit was just not attractive anymore. In fact, the child would turn its attention from the velveteen rabbit to newer and more modern toys.

Sometimes I feel professionals become like the velveteen rabbit. After years and years of service, whereas they were once the top professional and the key members of a delivery system, they became worn and tired and they're not the favorite of the client any longer. What we know to be true from the children's story and true about our adult life, is the velveteen rabbit was the first love and the favorite toy of the child. As the years go on the child may forget the velveteen rabbit.

In our professional and personal world it is important we stay diversified. The diversification of the individual is critical. The reclaiming of our personal and professional attraction is crucial in today's society. It is a society that has become so incredibly fast-paced. Think of all your colleagues and all the different careers, everyone is rushed, in a hurry and having to make decisions at a record pace. It's easy to become a velveteen rabbit. As we tire, it is more likely that we will be replaced by a younger, more modern toy. If we diversify our efforts and accept new challenges, we, in fact, become less stressed and more rejuvenated and energized. It is easier for us then to stay the favorite toy of the client, to stay on top for a longer period of time because we bring to the game a new, modern and exciting vision for the client. We, as professionals, do not have to go the way of the velveteen rabbit. If we were cared for and loved once, we can be again if we bring something new to the game.

XXXIII

THE RACE

XXXIII

THE RACE

Marketing and sales are often referred to as a race with no finish line.

R emember earlier when I said to try to be as good as your children think you are? One particular day, that just did not happen for me. It was the first 5k running race I had ever entered. The race was being held to benefit children with special needs on a very flat course close to our office building. I was a bit nervous yet excited to be in my first race. My son, Anthony, Jr., who was nine years old at the time and my wife, Linda, were due to arrive at the finish line sometime after the start of the race.

The gun went off and off we went. I realized in a hurry the humbling part of running or participating in any sport is there is always someone faster and someone slower. As is true in any running race, the speed burners had taken off and had finished the race in sixteen minutes or so. What I didn't realize was that Anthony, Jr. was questioning Linda as he saw the earlier finishers coming in as to where his dad was. Linda reminded him to look at the clock as it was not near the time I would be finishing, which would be closer to my "steady" twenty-four minutes. As I rounded the corner I could see my wife and son just beyond the finish line so I mustered the best final sprint I could. As I huffed and puffed across the finish line, my son walked towards me. As I was bent over sucking air, he looked deeply in my eyes and said, "Dad, where have you been?"

Just like running a race or in marketing or any profession, there are people who are going to ask, "Where have we been? Why have we not delivered on their expectations?" Anthony, Jr. certainly expected me to either win the race or finish near the top. Of course, I had the young boy stand around and witness that there were a few other people still out there on the course. But, I think the lesson we have to learn, whether it is in athletics or any area of new challenge or achievement, is, in creating reality, the truth is there is always someone faster or slower, brighter or more talented than we may be.

Our goal in business or any endeavor is to do our best and attempt to excel whenever possible. As the saying goes, the only failure is not trying.

XXXIV

THE FALL TO FOREVER

XXXIV

THE FALL TO FOREVER

I t was lunchtime at the construction site and we were all sitting around joking and complaining about the heat. The laborers were busy completing the scaffolding for our crew to climb and work on the next level of the building.

Greg and I finished our lunch and began to climb the scaffold. Once we reached the top, somewhere around forty feet high, I walked across the top tier of planking. What I didn't know until it was too late was that the laborers had overlapped two planks without the proper security. When I reached that portion of planking I crashed through and began to fall. I threw my hands above my head praying to grab onto anything solid. As I felt the panic strike me, Greg grabbed my hand and wrist from above me. I recall looking into his eyes and seeing his pain from holding my weight. I pleaded with him not to drop me. He gave a half smile and urged me to reach for the side of the scaffold. It seemed like an eternity, but we managed to reach the metal cross rod.

It was, for me, a fall to forever because it will always guide my thinking and feelings. That experience over twenty years ago, has guided me more in decisions than any boardroom battle I ever encountered. I believe the role of the leader is to catch the falling colleague until he can secure himself. At times in the past, I have been criticized for hanging on too long to falling colleagues. I hoped they would reach above their heads and take hold. I believe the fall from dignity and self-esteem is as dangerous as the fall from a building. Believe, with me, you can make a grab for a falling friend, colleague or yourself. You can make a difference, achieve impossible goals, dream a new dream and, above all else, remember you can CREATE REALITY.

"I REALIZED THE ROAD TO PERSONAL ACCOMPLISHMENT TRAVELS THROUGH A TUNNEL OF REALITY LIT BY HARD WORK, DEDICATION AND A PASSION TO MAKE A DIFFERENCE TO ME AND OTHERS."

– Anthony C. Gruppo

Special appreciation for their professionalism.
Anne Henshaw, Denise Shirk and Jim Wagner

GOALS AND DREAMS

_____

_____

_____

_____

_____

_____

_____

_____

_____

_____

_____

_____

_____

_____

_____

_____

_____

_____

_____

_____

_____

_____

_____

_____

_____

_____

_____

_____

_____

_____

_____